ACKNOWLEDGEMENTS

I have to start by thanking my wife Bimbo for spending endless nights editing & proof reading this book whilst dealing with work, ministry & the home front. How she does it I don't know but I have literally run out of words to express my gratitude.

I must appreciate & thank Kike Fadeyi for undertaking the initial proofreading of the manuscript. I also want to thank Tolu Adesina, Yemisi Ayeni & Kemi Faloye for taking on the task of doing the final proof read at breakneck speed.

Thanks once more to Tunde Adewumi for coordinating the project & Bayo Awe for dealing with operations logistics partly whilst on honeymoon.

For all those who have let me use their examples albeit anonymously thank you for making the book so practical.

Finally I have to thank my sons for allowing me chunks of their "daddy time" to get this resource out there. I love you boys & you will forever remain my number one priority.

DEDICATION

"Here am I and the children whom the LORD has given me! We are for signs and wonders in Israel " – Isaiah 8:18

I dedicate this book to my Natural Sons, Toni and Tola for sacrificing precious time with their Dad as they allow me to spend endless hours reading, praying and writing, and days and weekends and sometimes weeks away from home travelling and impacting other people for God. May the God I serve keep and watch over you. May our sacrifices speak for us with God for eternity! May it count for many generations to come!

I also dedicate this book to the many Spiritual Sons and Daughters I have raised and that will be raised by the message in this book, may you become all that God has destined you to be and grow to become God's friend such that you can overhear the secret conversations going on in heaven My prayer is that you will be responsible and faithful with what God has committed to your hands and remain faithful until the very end.

CONTENT

PREFACE

WHY THIS BOOK?

"It is the glory of God to <u>conceal a thing</u>: but the honour of kings is to <u>search out a matter</u>."- Prov. 25:2

There is a great hunger in the world for answers to questions and a yearning for real solutions to long standing problems. People are desperate to know who they are, why they are here, where they will end up and what the future holds.

The quest for answers and solutions to life's problems and the worlds' mysteries has led many along different paths and distant journeys. Some have travelled the road of science for lasting solutions to life's puzzles, whilst others have forayed into philosophy in search of answers to life's toughest questions. For many, religion has been the path that they have followed in a desire to find real peace and harmony. The current trend for some is the way of ancient mystics and exploring the occult in search of power to solve problems or find meaning and purpose in life. Unfortunately, many of these routes may at best only yield temporary relief. The real answers to life and solutions to its many problems can only ultimately be found in one place – in the mind of God, the Creator.

An old African proverb illustrates the point well in the saying,

"What you went looking for all the way in Tokyo has been hiding nearby in your Trouser pocket"!

Yes, indeed, the answers to the questions we ask and the solutions we seek have always been hidden in the mind of our Creator and the only way we can access it is by developing a real and genuine relationship with Him.

If you had a problem with your Dell computer, there is no sense in asking the carpenter or plumber down the road to fix it because they did not manufacture your computer, neither are they trained to deal with computers. The best way to fix the problem with your computer is to go to Mr Michael Dell himself who knows why he made the computer, what he put in it, why he put it in and how to fix it; or you can go to an authorised dealer to ask for the help of a computer technician.

Genuine Products in the hands of Fraudulent Men
Unfortunately, there are a lot of fictitious and pretentious unauthorised people posing as "repair men" to whom millions of unsuspecting people go to when their life malfunctions.
Multitudes will keep falling into their hands and be defrauded by them because there is a real shortage of trained and authorised "computer repair men".

"For they have <u>healed the hurt</u> of the daughter of my people <u>slightly (Superficially), Saying, 'Peace, peace!' When there is no peace</u>… Is there <u>no balm in Gilead</u>, Is there <u>no physician there</u>? Why then is there <u>no recovery</u> for the health of the daughter of my people?"
Jer. 8:11 & 22

There is a proliferation of psychics in the world and false prophets in the church who are proffering false solutions to desperate people whose lives are malfunctioning and are falling apart.

"Thus says the LORD of hosts: "Do not listen to the words of the prophets who prophesy to you. They make you worthless; they speak a vision of their own heart, not from the mouth of the LORD... "I have not sent these prophets, yet they ran. I have not spoken to them, yet they prophesied."- Jer23:16 & 21

There is a Shortage of Real Prophets

In the passage below, we see that Jesus exemplifies the need to help identify and deal with people's problems and recurrent trends. He helped identify and solve the problem by His access to supernatural revelation and power.

15 "The woman said to Him, "Sir, give me this water, that I may not thirst, nor come here to draw."
16 Jesus said to her, "Go, call your husband and come here."
17 The woman answered and said, "I have no husband." Jesus said to her, "You have well said, 'I have no husband,'
18 "for you have had five husbands and the one whom you now have is not your husband; in that you spoke truly."
19 The woman said to Him, "Sir, I perceive that You are a prophet."- John 4:15-19

The above scripture shows the importance of supernatural insight in unveiling what is at the root of people's problems. Given the high demand for answers to tough questions and lasting solutions to malfunctioning lives, I have written this book. My aim is that through this book people would, in a user-friendly way, be equipped to access supernatural revelations and solutions and the prophetic life. My overriding desire is to make the ability to hear and know the plans and will of God for us as individuals easy and accessible to all.

Do you understand Computer Language?

In my early teens while I was on a long summer break, my father enrolled me in a 3 week computer school run by an Apple computer dealer on Apple Macintosh computers. The school was designed to help us learn computer language so we could understand and create programs ourselves since this was required to operate computers in the early 1980s.

The class was somewhat tedious and often confusing. We had to learn words and commands like "GOSUB", GOTO", "SYNTAX ERROR" and suchlike. To operate a computer at that time, one had to learn these commands as they were required to run simple programs. The use of an Apple computer was limited to a very select and learned few at the time, until Steve Jobs the CEO and Co-founder of Apple inc. came up with the design of user-friendly computers a few years later which did not require any knowledge of programming. He ushered in the computer with a friendly, colourful, pictorial interface with "icons" that symbolised various commands and that were easy to navigate. In so doing, Steve Jobs made the use of computers accessible to all with Bill Gates taking it further at a later stage with the creation of his Windows interface as the Operating System for most other computers.

This book in a nutshell, is an attempt to simplify "spiritual language" by giving you "icons" or an understanding of spiritual symbology so that hearing God becomes easy and accessible to you.

God speaks in coded (locked) language

God hides things away for us, but not from us and releases or reveals these things at the appointed time in His own way in order to ensure the enemy is unable to access and thwart His plans for us.

8 "But we speak the wisdom of God in a <u>mystery, the hidden wisdom</u> <u>which God ordained before the ages for our glory,</u> 8 which none of the rulers of this age knew; <u>for had they known,</u> they would not have crucified the Lord of glory.
9 But as it is written: <u>Eye has not seen, nor ear heard, Nor have entered</u> <u>into the heart of man the things which God has prepared for those who</u> <u>love Him."</u>
10 But <u>God has revealed them to us through His Spirit</u>. For the Spirit searches all things, yes, the deep things of God... These things we also speak, not in words which man's wisdom teaches but which <u>the Holy</u> <u>Spirit teaches</u>, comparing spiritual things with spiritual."- 1Cor. 2:8-10 & 13

It is quite evident that God speaks in mysteries (coded or locked language) which can only be accessed by the discerning and enlightened. However, when He wants to speak to one of His own, He teaches them His "computer language" so that they can understand how He communicates and what He is saying.

"But the <u>natural man does not receive the things of the Spirit of God,</u> for they are <u>foolishness to him;</u> nor can he know them, because <u>they are</u> <u>spiritually discerned."</u>1Cor. 2:14

In this book you will learn:
1. How God speaks
2. How to decode secrets
3. How to unlock God's mysteries concerning your life.

One of the many tools through which God communicates to all is the medium of dreams. Almost every single person has had at least one dream in their life time. God speaks to all human beings but most people don't understand His language hence there is a need to ask God for the power of revelation when things that were previously concealed by Him are revealed to us.

The Power of Revelation

God speaks and has spoken in many ways in times past - through dreams, visions, parables, as well as spoken and written prophecies. As seen in the following passages we can see that messages that were previously locked, coded and concealed can be opened, unveiled and revealed in order to access important messages given to us by God for our advantage for a specific time and purpose.

""But you, Daniel, <u>shut up the words and seal the book until the time of the end;</u> many shall run to and fro and knowledge shall increase.""-
Dan.12:4

"And he said to me, "<u>Do not seal the words of the prophecy of this book</u>, for <u>the time is at hand</u>."- Rev. 22:10

2 "In the first year of his reign I, Daniel, <u>understood by the books the number of the years specified by the word</u> of the LORD through Jeremiah the prophet, <u>that He would accomplish seventy years in the desolations of Jerusalem.</u>
3 Then I set my face toward the Lord God to make request by prayer and supplications, with fasting, sackcloth and ashes."- Dan.9:2-3

Every secret thing will be revealed.

Some things are kept secret or hidden in order to protect or preserve or to conceal a matter. Some people conceal past indiscretions or present demeanours. In this dispensation, do you know no secret can remain a secret forever?

""For there is <u>nothing hidden</u> which will not <u>be revealed</u>, nor has anything been <u>kept secret</u> but that it <u>should come to light</u>."- Mark 4:22

God knows every past secret, our present hidden struggles and our concealed future successes. In this book, we will teach you to access and unlock the crucial secret things and mysteries concerning your life and destiny and that of others God brings across your path and how to uncover the enemy's secret plots and foil them.

Enjoy the read!

Dr Sola Fola-Alade

SECTION 1

THE NEED FOR PROPHECY

CHAPTER ONE

WHY WE NEED REAL PROPHETS
PART 1

LOOKING FOR ANSWERS IN ALL THE WRONG PLACES

Many are looking for the right answers in the wrong place

For thousands of years and in almost every tribe on the face of the earth there is an insatiable quest to know what the future holds. Many are also curious about what lays behind the façade of people's pretentious smiles and desire to see deep into the recesses of their hearts.

People want to know whom they should marry or if a spouse is really faithful, where they should live and what job they should be doing, what to invest in or how the stock or property market will do in the next few months. Many have done (or are willing to do) anything to get this kind of knowledge - hence the proliferation of psychics, fortune-tellers and diviners.

Even science has gotten in on the act - it is the reason why lie detectors and x-ray machines were invented and are used daily. These machines have been designed to see what the natural eye or man cannot always discern. If Judges had supernatural knowledge, there would be no need for jurors, if doctors had supernatural insight there would be no use for radiological or chemical diagnostic tests and if the Police had supernatural information there would be no need for undercover agents. In the same vein, if individuals had supernatural insight and foresight, there would be fewer divorce cases, heartbreaks and broken homes.

Supernatural insight is evidently needed in the marketplace and in homes to bring light to dark situations and make for peace and prosperity in our communities and society as a whole. The importance of the awakening and development of prophetic abilities in as many believers as is feasible cannot be over-emphasised. We all need it and people in the world are desperate for Supernatural guidance and interventions.

The Psychic business is Big Business
Until recently, I thought psychics only existed in funfairs and gypsy settlements and that palm readings and gazing into a crystal ball were things of the past or practised only by a quirky few. I was proved wrong when my children pointed out a signboard advertising a psychic fair which was holding in a pub a few houses up the road from ours and I soon noticed a proliferation of them in other pubs, clubs and community halls around our neighbourhood.

My wife recently drew my attention to an advert by psychics in a monthly women's magazine dedicated to personal development and wellbeing.

The magazine is quite popular amongst young upwardly mobile professional women and is published and distributed in the United Kingdom, Italy, Spain, Russia, Romania and China and now in Mexico. The magazine had achieved a print run of over 320,000 copies in 2005.

The advert said,
KNOW YOUR FUTURE TODAY!
Get 10 minutes of spiritual insight for only £2.90

The organization claims to be the UK's most trusted live psychic service with over 13 years experience in selecting the most gifted and authentic psychic readers to answer clients' questions. They have over 300 hand selected and verified psychic readers to choose from and the client is protected by a 100% money back guarantee. The Founder says, "We came together out of a desire to offer sincere and trustworthy guidance to every day people seeking answers in their lives". She adds, "Our work is simple. If you have an unresolved issue in your life, our psychic readers will tap into the background, providing you with the information you need to move forward. By offering caring but honest insight, you'll get a clear view into your choices and an empowering opportunity to stop feeling 'stuck'. The rest is up to you."
They also put in testimonials from some clients to verify their claims, they read as follows;

"My recent reading with DM blew me away. <u>Within the first 5 minutes he hit the nail on the head without any prompting on my part</u>... I gained clarity about work and about an important relationship. It was

a full reading which made me stand back and think. As a 'spirit messenger' DM has the utmost confidence."- **Mike, Norwich**

"I was stunned. Joy described my boyfriend (Sagittarius, brown hair, light eyes, younger than me) and his little girl who she said wished we hadn't split up (true because his daughter did tell me that)... Joy gave me a brilliant insight into how my ex is feeling at the moment and what is going to happen in the future. She didn't waffle or ask leading questions. She just went straight to the point. I feel so much better and would definitely go back to her again. I just wish I had booked a longer session."- **Liz, Lancaster**

"Three and a half years ago, I lost my four and a half year old daughter tragically. It was a dreadful situation and I was utterly devastated. I am a practical person and desperately needed evidence of my daughter's survival in spirit. S gave a clear level of detail which no one could possibly have known. I have always felt to this day that my daughter chose him as a channel to communicate through. The messages brought me comfort and courage to continue with my life knowing my daughter is still around me. S continues to read accurately about the children I have now and my job."- **Julie, Dublin**

The real examples above are proof that psychics are really at work and are in high demand. The proliferation we see of psychics today is because of people's need for direction, hope, comfort, encouragement, connection, answers and solutions to desperate problems.

The Shocking Truth about Ronald and Nancy Reagan's Use of Psychic Help

I recently read an article on a blog with the above named title posted on the 29th of March 2009 on www.articlesbased.com. The article contents are paraphrased below:

Though shocking as the title indicates, it comes out as no secret at all to the fact that the Reagan presidency was actually controlled by the cosmos astrological forces.

It is believed that the Reagan's, while making very important decisions concerning the state and in the White House strongly relied on astrology as a saviour. Joan Quigley who was an astrologer, planned almost all presidential travel and press conferences, as well as Reagan's cancer surgery which she planned based on astrology. It is believed that one signing of a treaty between the U.S and the Soviet to eliminate the medium-range nuclear missiles was signed on astrological advice from Quigley: the treaty was signed on December 8, 1987 at 1.30 p.m. When Reagan was Governor of California, he signed a legislation that allowed licensed astrologers to practice their trade and removed them from the category of being fortune tellers. There is one astrologer known as Jeanne Dixon who became very famous because she predicted the assassination of President Kennedy and she was also an astrological advisor to the Reagan's. She predicted that Reagan would become Governor of California in 1962 and later the President of The U.S. Dixon gained Reagan's favor but was later dropped by Nancy when she predicted that the husband Reagan would not win the presidential elections in 1976 (she was correct).

Joyce Jillson was yet another astrologer who helped the Reagan's in selecting the vice president from a list of seven candidates. She suggested George Bush as the best candidate because Bush was a Gemini, which she deemed as the most compatible sign to Reagan who was an Aquarian.

In 1980, when Reagan commenced his campaign, another astrologer by the name Quigley came on the scene. Quigley had pointed out that March 30 would be a terrible day for Reagan and on March 30, 1981 there was an assassination attempt against Reagan. At this point, Quigley was promoted from being a casual astrologer friend to astrological protector for Reagan's life. It was around this time that Nancy Reagan also became aware of the so called "Presidential Death Cycle" (also known as the "Zero-year curse") by which every president elected at a particular time since the election of William Harrison has died while in office.

Wikipedia further corroborates this article with the facts below. Joan Quigley (born April 10, 1927), of San Francisco, is an astrologer best known for her astrological advice to the Reagan White House in the 1980s. Quigley was born in Kansas City, Missouri. She was called on by First Lady Nancy Reagan in 1981 after John Hinckley's attempted assassination of the president and stayed on as the White House astrologer in secret until being ousted in 1988 by former chief of staff Donald Regan.

These stories about the Reagan's is further proof that people are desperate for answers, guidance and direction regardless of their position or place in life and are willing to dabble into forbidden mystic and occult practices to get these answers. The passage below shows that these acts are clearly forbidden practices in the scriptures.

10*"There shall not be found among you anyone who makes his son or his daughter pass through the fire, or one who practices witchcraft, or a soothsayer, or one who interprets omens, or a sorcerer,*

11 *"or one who conjures spells, or a medium (psychic), or a spiritist, or one who calls up the dead.*

12 *"For all who do these things are an abomination to the LORD and because of these abominations the LORD your God drives them out from before you.*

13 "*You shall be blameless before the LORD your God.*

14 "*For these nations which you will dispossess listened to <u>soothsayers</u> and <u>diviners;</u> but as for you, the LORD your God has not appointed such for you.*

15 "*The LORD your <u>God will raise up for you a Prophet</u> like me from your midst, from your brethren. <u>Him you shall hear</u>,...*"*- Deut. 18:10-15*

GOD WANTS AND NEEDS MORE PROPHETIC PEOPLE

Moses' desire for more prophets

God's answer to this age old problem has always been to raise authentic prophets. With the proliferation of psychics and mediums and with the level of desperation in the world for answers and an intense desire for the supernatural, there is a great demand for true prophets. Could that be why in both the old and new testaments both Moses and Paul wished there were more prophets?

"... *Then Moses said to him, "Are you zealous for my sake? Oh, <u>that all the LORD'S people were prophets</u> and <u>that the LORD would put His Spirit upon them</u>!*" "*- Num. 11:29*

Perhaps, because of the great need and demand that Moses saw with individuals desperately seeking supernatural answers to their every day problems such that they sought for answers with diviners and mediums as we see today, he desired a multiplication of the prophetic gift and that God pours His Spirit on all and make them a prophetic people.

Paul's desire for more people to prophesy

Paul also expressed a similar desire to Moses in that he also wished in his own time that everyone would prophesy. He encouraged everyone to earnestly desire the gift of prophesy.

"...5 I wish you all spoke with tongues, but even more that you prophesied; for he who prophesies is greater than he who speaks with tongues, unless indeed he interprets, that the church may receive edification... "- 1 Corinthians 14:5

Beyond what the eyes can see

Not only are true leaders like Moses and Paul calling for a prophetic generation, the people seek it too.

There is a new generation of believers arising that are no longer content with just walking by their five natural senses of sight, sound, smell, taste and touch. This is a generation that hungers and thirsts for supernatural knowledge, insights and divinely granted information into realms previously inaccessible to man.

"Where there is no revelation, the people cast off restraint; but happy is he who keeps the law"- Prov. 29:18

Where there is no divine revelation people lack real discipline and live below their real potential, but those who have access to it walk at a higher level of provision, protection and honour. That is what you are called to.

How God trains His Prophets (Eagles)

I feel God has called me to awaken the church and train it into its prophetic responsibilities - to become sharper, keener and more spiritually and naturally vigilant. To make the church more focused in its assignment and objectives and to raise it to demonstrate God's majesty, power and His Spirit of Excellence in character, in execution and in exploits.

10""He found him in a desert land and in the wasteland, a howling wilderness; He encircled him, He instructed him, He kept him as the apple of His eye.

11 As an eagle stirs up its nest, Hovers over its young, Spreading out its wings, taking them up, Carrying them on its wings,

12 So the LORD alone led him and there was no foreign god with him.

13 "He made him ride in the heights of the earth, that he might eat the produce of the fields; He made him draw honey from the rock and oil from the flinty rock;"- Deut. 32:10 -13

Expect Prophetic Rain over Cities

"And it shall come to pass afterward That I will pour out My Spirit on all flesh; Your sons and your daughters shall prophesy, Your old men shall dream dreams, Your young men shall see visions."- Joel 2:28

On the 25th of Feb 2011, while I was worshipping, the Lord showed me a picture of a Heavy Rain of His Spirit being poured upon multitudes of people to bring Supernatural revelation and raise Prophetic Watchmen over their territory (Family, Neighbourhood, Community, City and Nation). These people will be so spiritually sensitive that they will be able to pick up and intercede against events like September 11 all over the World.

"17 And I will come down and talk with you there; and I will take of the Spirit which is upon you and will put It upon them; and they shall bear the burden of the people with you, so that you may not have to bear it yourself alone…. Then the LORD came down in the cloud and spoke to him and took some of the spirit that was upon him and put it upon the seventy elders; and when the spirit rested upon them, they prophesied. But they did so no more. "Numbers 11:17, 25

You shall no longer grope in the dark

""And _you shall grope_ at noonday, _as a blind man gropes in darkness;_ you shall not prosper in your ways; _you shall be only oppressed_ and _plundered continually_ and no one shall save you."- Deut. 28:29

The above scripture indicates that one can have perfect natural eyesight and still grope in the dark in the noonday but God desires supernatural sight for His people.

Transforming Ostriches into Eagles

Approximately 21 years ago, I saw the vision of an ostrich with its head buried in the sand. This mother ostrich began to lay 12 eggs around the circumference of a circle where it stood in the centre in the middle of the desert. As I looked up, I saw an army of invaders approaching from some oil rich countries in the Middle East trying to destroy the baby ostriches that had just recently hatched but the mother ostrich was totally oblivious to all that was happening.

I believe it is quite instructive that God chooses to use a bird like the proverbial ostrich, with its _"head buried in the sand"_ to describe the church in this vision. The ostrich is a bird that is often totally oblivious to what is happening around it in spite of near and present danger.

Many years later, God told me that He has called me to raise an Eagle generation of believers. Eagles are like the opposite of Ostriches. Eagles are very intelligent, focused and vigilant birds that are very protective, nurturing and take delight in training their young for extra-ordinary flight at 33,000ft. Eagles have incredible focus and "far-sight" - they can see a reptile as far as 2 miles away. They are territorial birds and are very protective and watchful over their terrain. They are birds of prey that can be trained to hunt. They can live for as long as 80 years. They are extra-ordinary birds and they symbolise the Prophet.

Raising Prophetic Watchmen in every Home and Territory

1"Again the word of the LORD came to me, saying,
2 "Son of man, speak to the children of your people and say to them: <u>*'When I bring the sword upon a land*</u> *and the people of the land* <u>*take a man from their territory*</u> *and* <u>*make him their watchman,*</u>
3 <u>'when he sees the sword coming upon the land</u>, if he blows the trumpet and warns the people,..."-Ezek33:1-3

The Eagle is a very vigilant and watchful bird. My intention is to train people to become spiritually sensitive to things happening or about to happen to them, their family (or neighbourhood or sphere of influence) so that they can break negative spiritual trends, intercede and intervene in impeding satanic assaults and plans before they hatch. I shall discuss this in more detail later on in this book. Just imagine if someone had picked up the plot to bomb the World Trade Centre (Twin towers) in New York before September 11 2001 and raised people to intercede against that devastating attack? So much heartbreak, loss of life and economic damage could have been avoided. As you move from being an ostrich into an eagle, you will have godly influence over the circumstances of your life and those of others.

The 'Occasional' versus 'Occupational' Prophecy

Now I know that you may be thinking, 'Me, a prophet'? Let me reassure you a little – we are all called to prophecy even though we are not all prophets.

What is the difference between people who can prophesy and an actual prophet?

We cannot compare a novice who can successfully assemble an

IKEA bookshelf with the aid of a DIY manual to someone who studied carpentry at a technical school for a few years and who owns a professional joinery shop. Neither can we compare a school teacher who applies an icepack to reduce external swelling on a child who is hit on the head with a hockey stick to a trained Neurosurgeon who has had years of highly technical training and who can perform a 6 hour operation to remove a subdural haematoma (internal bleeding) in order to save the child's life. In the same light, all can prophesy, but not all are prophets i.e. all can access a fragment of God's mind concerning a situation supernaturally on occasions but not all are called to occupy the position and office of a Prophet where they do it regularly and as a calling. You may not be a prophet but you are called to be prophetic.

CHAPTER 2

WHY WE NEED REAL PROPHETS PART II

DISCOVERING THE KING IN YOU (UNVEILING WHO YOU REALLY ARE)

"Now the <u>LORD had told Samuel in his ear the day before Saul came</u>, saying,
16 "Tomorrow about this time <u>I will send you a man</u> from the land of Benjamin and <u>you shall anoint him commander over My people</u> Israel, that he may save My people from the hand of the Philistines; for I have looked upon My people, because their cry has come to me."
17 And <u>when Samuel saw Saul, the LORD said to him, "There he is, the man of whom I spoke to you. This one shall reign over my people."</u>
18 Then Saul drew near to Samuel in the gate and said, "Please tell me, <u>where is the seer's house?"</u>
19 And Samuel answered Saul and said, <u>"I am the seer."</u>- 1 Sam 9:15-19

Over the years, I have come to the conclusion that there is more to each individual than meets the eye and that you can never really know who is sitting or standing next to you by using your natural senses alone. As humans, we tend to judge a book by its cover, but to every human life, there are many yet unread and unwritten volumes to their lives. Prophecy can also help us understand who we are and what we are called to.

History & Destiny

Every human being we meet and relate with has both a history and a destiny. If we care to take time to ask questions, every individual has a fascinating history that dates back many generations. I shook a gentleman by the hand when he walked into the church I pastored a few years back and decided to have a conversation beyond the usual superficial greetings and routine exchanges. After a few minutes of asking questions in order to get to know him better, I discovered his late father was at one time Head of State (President) of a leading African nation. He had been killed in a military coup a few decades ago. He looked so simple and humble but he had a colourful, privileged and yet traumatic past that I could never have known just by looking or interacting superficially with him.

Just as we cannot always pick up a person's past by looking at them, we can often never judge a person's future (destiny) merely by observing their present circumstances. Who would have ever thought that the young man who flipped and sold hamburgers in a little fast food restaurant in Hawaii in the early 70's would one day become the president of the USA - President Barack Obama? I know of a Pastor who leads a large church (about 7,000 members) in Nigeria in West Africa. He used to be a drug addict who lived on the streets due to his drug habit. A decade or so earlier no one could have known how many lives he would touch with the gospel message. This is what the prophetic ministry is all about – enabling one to see both what is hidden from the past (insight) and what is to come in the future (foresight). We see this played out in scripture in the life of Saul.

" "*Now the <u>LORD had told Samuel in his ear the day before Saul came</u>, saying,*

16 "Tomorrow about this time <u>I will send you a man</u> from the land of Benjamin and <u>you shall anoint him commander over My people</u> Israel, that he may save My people from the hand of the Philistines; for I have looked upon My people, because their cry has come to me."

17 And <u>when Samuel saw Saul, the LORD said to him, "There he is, the man of whom I spoke to you. This one shall reign over my people."</u>"- 1 Sam 9:15-17

Saul was looking for sheep but God was speaking of his destiny as a king to Samuel.

Roots and Fruit

Like the scripture indicates, men are indeed like trees (Psalm 1:1-3) , in that when you see a man standing in front of you, what you see is not all there is to him or her. There is more to them than meets the eye. Just like every tree has a root system that lies hidden beneath the surface of the ground it stands on; in the same vein, every man or woman we meet has a history or root system which makes them who they are. It is called their genealogy or heritage.

The scripture below traces 42 generations between Jesus Christ and Abraham.

"The book of the genealogy of Jesus Christ, the Son of David, the Son of Abraham:

2 Abraham begot Isaac, Isaac begot Jacob and Jacob begot Judah and his brothers.

3 Judah begot Perez and Zerah by Tamar, Perez begot Hezron and Hezron begot Ram.

4 Ram begot Amminadab, Amminadab begot Nahshon and Nahshon begot Salmon.

5 Salmon begot Boaz by Rahab, Boaz begot Obed by Ruth, Obed begot Jesse,

6 and Jesse begot David the king. David the king begot Solomon by her who had been the wife of Uriah.

7 Solomon begot Rehoboam, Rehoboam begot Abijah and Abijah begot Asa.

8 Asa begot Jehoshaphat, Jehoshaphat begot Joram and Joram begot Uzziah.

9 Uzziah begot Jotham, Jotham begot Ahaz and Ahaz begot Hezekiah.

10 Hezekiah begot Manasseh, Manasseh begot Amon and Amon begot Josiah.

11 Josiah begot Jeconiah and his brothers about the time they were carried away to Babylon.

12 And after they were brought to Babylon, Jeconiah begot Shealtiel and Shealtiel begot Zerubbabel.

13 Zerubbabel begot Abiud, Abiud begot Eliakim and Eliakim begot Azor.

14 Azor begot Zadok, Zadok begot Achim and Achim begot Eliud.

15 Eliud begot Eleazar, Eleazar begot Matthan and Matthan begot Jacob.

16 And Jacob begot Joseph the husband of Mary, of whom was born Jesus who is called Christ.

17 So all the generations from <u>Abraham to David</u> are <u>fourteen generations</u>, from David until the captivity in Babylon are fourteen generations and from the captivity in Babylon until the Christ are fourteen generations."- Matt. 1:1-17

Generational Blessings or Curses

Why is this important to us and our lives today? It is because our history can affect our destiny. In the medical field, when a patient comes to the clinic with a headache, chest pain or fever, the doctor is expected to take a full medical history regardless of the symptoms the patient is complaining of. The doctor must also ask the patient for his family and social history i.e. whether the patient's parents suffered from diabetes or hypertension. The doctor takes this history because medicine recognises that some medical conditions are inherited.

"Now as Jesus passed by, He saw a man who was <u>blind from birth</u>. 2 And His disciples asked Him, saying, "Rabbi, <u>who sinned, this man</u> or <u>his parents</u>, that he <u>was born blind?</u>""-John 9:1

Just as we can inherit medical conditions from our parents, our forebears' sin can either be passed down or influence our destiny negatively.

"You shall not bow down to them nor serve them. For I, the LORD your God, am a jealous God, <u>visiting</u> the <u>iniquity of the fathers</u> on <u>the children</u> to the <u>third and fourth generations</u> of those who hate Me,"- Exodus 20:4

This shows that according to the law of God, a person's sin or iniquity can influence up to four generations of that individual (that is approximately 32 persons in his genealogy).

The same is true concerning the blessings that may come as regards the good deeds of our forbears being passed down to succeeding generations.

"...but showing <u>mercy</u> to <u>thousands</u>, to those who <u>love Me</u> and keep <u>My commandments</u>." Exodus 20:5
"7 So David said to him, "Do not fear, for I will surely <u>show you kindness</u>

for Jonathan your <u>father's sake</u> and will restore to you all the land of Saul your grandfather; and you shall eat bread at my table continually." "- 2 Sam.9:7

These spiritual truths show that a person's life or destiny can be positively or negatively affected by their forebears. The prophetic ministry has the ability to see and unveil the root causes of the issues people face and are struggling with today.

What about your future?

Not only does the prophetic ministry look back at history and explores the root, it also looks forward into an individual's destiny and looks at their potential.

Seed potential

"And behold, the LORD stood above it and said: "I <u>am the LORD God of Abraham your father and the God of Isaac;</u> the land on which you <u>lie I will give to you and your descendants.</u>

14 "Also your descendants shall be as the dust of the earth; you shall spread abroad to the west and the east, to the north and the south; and <u>in you and in your seed all the families of the earth shall be blessed.</u>

15 "Behold, I am with you and will keep you wherever you go and will bring you back to this land; for I will not leave you until I have done what I have spoken to you."

16 Then Jacob awoke from his sleep and said, "Surely the LORD is in this place and I did not know it." "- Gen. 28: 13-16

If I placed a seed in my hand and asked you the question, "What do you see?" your response will be dependent on how prophetic you are.

If your answer is, "A seed", it means you judge with your <u>Natural-Sight;</u>

If it is, "A tree with fruit", then you have a measure of <u>Foresight;</u>
But if it is, "A forest or an orchard", you definitely have <u>Far-sight.</u>

Just like a seed has a potential to become a forest, when God looks at a man or woman, He sees far beyond the man and sees the millions of people who will come from his loins or her womb.

"And they blessed Rebekah and said to her: "Our sister, may you become the mother of thousands of ten thousands; and may your descendants possess the gates of those who hate them.""- Gen. 24:60

""And He has made from <u>one blood</u> (one man) <u>every nation of men</u> to dwell on all the face of the earth and has determined their pre-appointed times and the boundaries of their dwellings,"-Acts17:26

Who are you and what is your purpose?
When I meet people I tend to look beyond who I see in front of me. I tend to ask these questions in my mind, 'Who is this person really?' 'What will they become in 20 years?', 'What is the purpose for their life?' or 'What will their children or grand-children become?'

Jesus saw a potential evangelist in a serial divorcee.
Who are you really and what on earth are you here for? I have come to see that there can be a prime minister in a pauper, a deacon in a drug addict, a lawyer in a prostitute and a CEO in a cleaner. The only way to find out is by asking the Creator the purpose for each creation.

""Thus says the LORD who made it, the LORD who formed it to establish it (the LORD is His name):
3 '<u>Call to Me</u> and <u>I will answer you</u> and <u>show you</u> <u>great and mighty things,</u> which you do not know.'"- Jer. 33:2-3

CHAPTER 3

WHY WE NEED REAL PROPHETS
PART III

Unveiling Beauty or the Beast (Revealing the Real Identity and Destiny of Others)

What if every single one of us had supernatural insight into the past lives, present secrets and future destinies of the people we come across and have to deal with? I believe we would have fewer divorces, business failures and church splits. The secret thoughts, hidden motives and agendas of people we interact with would be revealed and we would be able to wisely manage those personal and business relationships to minimise damage. This is another reason we need real prophets.

Before you choose your Partner

God still reveals the secrets of men's hearts to those who walk closely with Him and acknowledge Him in all their ways.

"Trust in the LORD with all your heart and <u>lean not on your own understanding;</u>
6 In <u>all your ways acknowledge Him</u> and <u>He shall direct your paths.</u>
7 <u>Do not be wise in your own eyes;</u> Fear the LORD and <u>depart from evil.</u>"- Prov. 3:5-6

The above passage has been a guiding light for me in the last twenty one years or so. This principle has saved and preserved me from many calamities in various romantic, ministry and business relationships. Early on in my walk with God, I was instructed through the admonition of the above scripture not to trust only in my five natural senses, my logical reasoning and mental faculties. Rather, I have learnt to lean on God, because God can see better, farther and clearer into every situation than I can; indeed, He knows every thought and intention of people's hearts. Do you know you can really have access to information about your future, as well as other people's secret sins, concealed past indiscretions and future tragic events through supernatural means? God reveals not because He is a gossip but in order to bring correction and healing.

Beauty is only skin deep

With this understanding as a single young man, even though I was on occasion attracted to and almost drawn away by the way some women looked, dressed or comported themselves; this scripture was a guide which reined me in from getting too close to or making commitments to those who I thought would make a good partner purely by observation.

With this scriptural understanding, as soon as I met a person I liked and thought I had feelings for, I always retreated and took it before the Lord before there was a chance for any attachments to develop. The benefits of doing this have proven to be extremely invaluable.

As a result, God would often open up their "personal files" to me showing me who they really were, what they had done, what they were involved in, what they were keeping back and what they would become in the future. Sometimes, all He said was *"Do not be unequally yoked"* or just, *"Get away from there!"* I cannot even begin to tell you how many calamities I was saved from as a result.

"Now the LORD said to Samuel, "How long will you mourn for Saul, seeing I have rejected him from reigning over Israel? Fill your horn with oil and go; I am sending you to Jesse the Bethlehemite. For I have provided Myself a king among his sons.""- 1 Sam. 16:1

The verse above further buttresses my point that indeed God can direct our decision making and rule out or reject one person over another either because of what they have done wrong or they may be blameless but might not be best suited for you or God may have someone else in mind for them (or you).

All that Glitters is not gold

We must live our lives in a way that pleases God, so that if any one makes an enquiry about us before God, we will have a good report before God. Scripture confirms that God has an opinion on every individual and can reveal it to us if He thinks we need to know or if the information will help us.

"So it was, when they came, that he looked at Eliab and said, "Surely the LORD'S anointed is before Him."
7 But the LORD said to Samuel, "Do not look at his appearance or at the height of his stature, because I have refused him. For the LORD does

not see as man sees; <u>for man looks at the outward appearance,</u> but <u>the LORD looks at the heart."</u>

8 So Jesse called Abinadab and made him pass before Samuel. And he said, <u>"Neither has the LORD chosen this one."</u>

9 Then Jesse made Shammah pass by. And he said, <u>"Neither has the LORD chosen this one."</u>

10 Thus Jesse made seven of his sons pass before Samuel. And Samuel said to Jesse, "The LORD has not chosen these."

11 And Samuel said to Jesse, "Are all the young men here?" Then he said, "There remains yet the youngest and there he is, keeping the sheep." And Samuel said to Jesse, <u>"Send and bring him. For we will not sit down till he comes here."</u>

12 So he sent and brought him in. Now he was ruddy, with bright eyes and good-looking. And the LORD said, <u>"Arise, anoint him; for this is the one!"</u>

13 Then Samuel took the horn of oil and anointed him in the midst of his brothers; and the Spirit of the LORD came upon David from that day forward. So Samuel arose and went to Ramah."-1 Sam. 16:6-13

God sometimes rejects, refuses or recommends people

God rejected Saul, refused Eliab, did not choose Abinadab, Shammah and the four other brothers, but chose David. In the same vein, when we are considering marriage, business or career opportunities, we must ask God for His opinion. This is a key way in which the prophetic can help in your day to day life and dealings.

Do you really know who you are living with?

By now I believe we have established that we cannot know all about people by just observing them through our five natural senses. There is more to them than meets the eye. Even our spouses are not fully known by us. Only God truly knows who each person is and where they are at in their heart.

Snakes in the marital bed

A certain lady had mentioned to me on one of our marriage retreats, that before she found out that her husband had being sexually unfaithful she had on a number of occasions had dreams where she saw snakes lying on their marital bed. It was only when her husband confessed that she concluded with prophetic hindsight that God had being trying to reveal the situation to her through her dreams about snakes.

Past secret revealed

One man also recounted dreams in which he saw his wife playing in a bed with a number of different men he could not recognize. His wife later told him that they were people she had being sexually intimate with prior to their marriage. She had not disclosed this for many years for fear of losing him as he had been led to believe that he was the only one she had been sexually intimate with. God reveals in order to expose a person when they are in a dangerous situation and haven't changed after numerous warnings or when it is necessary to bring healing to the situation.

Satan's plot uncovered and foiled

I also know of an instance in which God revealed an impending affair in a dream to an unsuspecting spouse. God did so in order to warn of an attack on the marriage and so that the couple could intercede and take necessary precautions. As a result, an inappropriate non-sexual relationship which had ensued was stopped from progressing further and a marriage and family were saved.

Spiritual Espionage - The evil they do in secret

"Then the <u>Spirit lifted me up and brought me to the East Gate of the LORD'S house</u>, which faces eastward; and there at the door of the gate

*were twenty-five men, among whom I saw Jaazaniah the son of Azzur
and Pelatiah the son of Benaiah, princes of the people.*
  *2 And He said to me: "Son of man, <u>these are the men who devise
iniquity and give wicked counsel in this city,</u>"*- Ezek. 11:1-3

The above passage shows that God reveals things that happen
with people who hold public office. While staying at a friend's
place in the U.S, I had a dream about the personal life of a high
public officer in the state he lived in. It was only a couple of
months later that it was revealed that the individual was indeed
involved in what I had seen.

There is no such thing as a Secret!

I have spent the night at other people's houses and without
asking God any questions He has chosen to reveal something
they had concealed which they were struggling with. God
unveiled it because He wanted to heal the individual of the sting
and guilt of the sin.

God reveals things happening 6000 miles away

While away on a foreign preaching engagement, God revealed to
me in a dream that a certain single lady who was then a member
of the church I led, was having indiscriminate sexual
relationships. On my return, during a miracle service, I
remembered the incident and whispered quietly in her ears what
I had seen. She confessed that she had picked up a stranger
earlier that day at a bus stop and had been sexually intimate with
him. She then repented and was restored in her walk with God.
God is to be feared. He sees all things.

*"19 Then <u>the secret was revealed to Daniel in a night vision</u>. So Daniel
blessed the God of heaven.*
  20 Daniel answered and said: "Blessed be the name of God forever and

ever, for wisdom and might are His.

21 And He changes the times and the seasons; <u>He removes kings and raises up kings</u>; He gives wisdom to the wise and knowledge to those who have understanding.

22 <u>He reveals deep and secret things</u>; He knows what is in the darkness and light dwells with Him."-Dan2:19-22

Are you wearing filthy garments?

"And it was told Tamar, saying, "Look, your father-in-law is going up to Timnah to shear his sheep."

14 <u>So she took off her widow's garments</u>, <u>covered herself with a veil and wrapped herself and sat in an open place</u> which was on the way to Timnah; for she saw that Shelah was grown and she was not given to him as a wife.

15 <u>When Judah saw her, he thought she was a harlot, because she had covered her face.</u>

16 Then he turned to her by the way and said, "Please let me come in to you"; for he did not know that she was his daughter-in-law. So she said, "What will you give me, that you may come in to me?""- Gen. 38:13-16

From the above passage, we can see that a decent looking person (widow) can steal away for a moment in their lives to enjoy a moment of indiscretion and the pleasures of sin, with the intention of resuming life as normal afterwards. From experience, I have seen that this incident can remain as a stain on one's spiritual garments. I have been able to pick up such things from some people's lives even though they thought they had walked away from such a moment and that it was behind them. Sin can leave an indelible stain or stench on one's life until we ask God to thoroughly cleanse us.

"Then he showed me Joshua the high priest standing before the Angel

of the LORD and <u>Satan standing at his right hand to oppose him.</u>
2 And the LORD said to Satan, "The LORD rebuke you, Satan! The
LORD who has chosen Jerusalem rebuke you! Is this not a brand
plucked from the fire?"
3 Now <u>Joshua was clothed with filthy garments</u> and was standing
before the Angel.

I have found over the years that sometimes, when people
experience some kind of spiritual hindrance or opposition in the
physical, it could be because of some un-confessed concealed sin
that Satan has on his record against them. As a result, just like
Joshua in this scripture, the enemy is then equipped to resist and
oppose them. A prophetic person who is sensitive to the spirit
and who God has chosen to intervene can pick these things up in
prayer and bring deliverance to the individual. As I said earlier,
God reveals secrets in order to bring correction and healing. His
revelations are often not punitive (to punish) but rather
redemptive.

4 Then He answered and spoke to those who stood before Him, saying,
"<u>Take away</u> the <u>filthy garments</u> from him." And to him He said, "See,
I <u>have removed your iniquity from you</u> and I will <u>clothe you with rich</u>
<u>robes</u>." "- Zech. 3:1-4

Beware of the spirit of Suspicion

As we close this chapter, it is important to note that although we
know God is a revealer of secrets, we should not go about
suspecting our spouses or other people if God has not of His own
volition revealed things to us. I do not want you to use the
prophetic as a door for introducing rancour into your
relationships. Remember that according to 1 Corinthians 13, love
believes the best of all people. The acid test of prophetic
revelation is that it must always be handled with maturity and

guided by love. Believe the best of people until you are clearly shown otherwise.

"...does not behave rudely, does not seek its own, is not provoked, thinks no evil;

6 does not rejoice in iniquity, but rejoices in the truth;

7 bears all things, believes all things, hopes all things, endures all things.

8 Love never fails. But whether there are prophecies, they will fail; whether there are tongues, they will cease; whether there is knowledge, it will vanish away.

9 For we know in part and we prophesy in part."-1Corinth13:5-9

SECTION 2

UNVEILING AND UNDERSTANDING THE PROPHETIC

CHAPTER 4

WHO IS A PROPHET?

A LAMP AND A LIGHT (REVEALER OF SECRETS)

A Prophet is a human agent that is appointed by a deity to function on His behalf as an intermediary on earth. He is divinely inspired to receive supernatural insights concerning people and their situations and predictive revelation concerning future earthly events.

A Prophet is one who is divinely endowed with the unique ability to receive, decode and effectively convey the divinely revealed messages to the chosen audience.

What problem do Prophets solve?

When you need a nail in the wall you get a hammer; if you need cool air you get a fan; if you need to see your way in darkness you get a torch. Whenever you need information to solve a problem you get a teacher or an expert in the field. In the same vein, when you need a secret revealed you look for a Prophet.

"3 Now the donkeys of Kish, Saul's father, were lost. And Kish said to his son Saul, "Please, take one of the servants with you and arise, go and look for the donkeys."
4 So he passed through the mountains of Ephraim and through the land of Shalisha, but they did not find them... And he said to him, "Look now, there is in this city a man of God and he is an honourable man; all that he says surely comes to pass. So let us go there; perhaps he can show us the way that we should go... 8 And the servant answered Saul again and said, "Look, I have here at hand one fourth of a shekel of silver. I will give that to the man of God, to tell us our way."
9 (Formerly in Israel, when a man went to inquire of God, he spoke thus: "Come, let us go to the seer"; for he who is now called a prophet was formerly called a seer.)
10 Then Saul said to his servant, "Well said; come, let us go." So they went to the city where the man of God was." "-1Sam9:1-6

God is a Problem Solver

God is not just a creator, He is also a solution provider and this means when He creates something and it gets broken He does something to fix it. When you buy a computer from a manufacturer or authorised dealer, it comes with a warranty that if it should ever malfunction, they will send a repair man with the necessary parts to fix it.

1"In the beginning God created the heavens and the earth.
2 The earth was without form and void; and darkness was on the face of the deep. And the Spirit of God was hovering over the face of the waters.
3 Then God said, "Let there be light"; and there was light."- Gen.1:1-3

Prophets are God's authorised repairmen with the right equipment and training to fix the problems of darkness on earth in every generation. They shed light where there is darkness.

The Revelatory Functions of a Prophet

There are two primary groupings of prophets; "Seeing" and "Hearing" Prophets. As we have already noted, one of the ways that God repairs or 'fixes' things is by giving prophets insight. Prophets who have see things afar off are 'seeing' prophets. We will look at this latter group in more details later through some of the activities of the Lord Jesus. Jesus is the greatest example of how a prophet should function and his responsibilities.

1.   Prophetic Insight

When Jesus met the Samaritan Woman at the well, after they had gone past the usual greetings, their conversation went a little deeper in that Jesus asked for her husband, but she responded by saying she had no husband.

> 15 *"The woman said to Him, "Sir, <u>give me this water, that I may not thirst,</u> nor come here to draw."*
> *16 Jesus said to her, "<u>Go, call your husband and</u> come here."*
> *17 The woman answered and said, "<u>I have no husband</u>." Jesus said to her, "You have well said, 'I have no husband,'*
> *18 "for you <u>have had five husbands and the one whom you now have is not your husband;</u> in that you spoke truly."*
> *19 The woman said to Him, "Sir, <u>I perceive that You are a prophet</u>."-*
> *John 4:14-19*

Was the woman's response a lie or the truth? At best, we can say she was very economical with the truth, perhaps because she was talking to a stranger. Jesus could not be waived off by that misrepresentation though. He went further and deeper to unveil the secrets of her heart and her past and present life. He revealed that she had been married and divorced five times and was either presently in adultery with another person's husband or at best living in with someone she was not married to. This is the powerful thing about prophetic insight – it unveils vital information that cannot be easily secured otherwise.

Such information can be vital in making the right decision on important matters. Walking in this kind of revelation can ensure for example that one does not make the wrong decision in the choice of a future partner. Prophetic insight helped me on several occasions not to marry the wrong person before I met my wife. I met a number of prospective partners who seemed to tick all the boxes but as I took their case before the Lord, He revealed things to me about them. Oftentimes, it was about things they had done in the past which they had not previously disclosed or things they were presently involved in which they had kept secret.

On one occasion, a certain Christian lady who I met at bible school (I guess you would think that was a great place for a pastor to meet his future wife) asked if she could come to see me in my office for a counselling appointment. She was good looking, well put together and elegant in carriage and I agreed to meet with her as requested. As was my practise, I prayed before the counselling appointment and then had a nap. As I awoke from my brief nap, I heard a clear audible voice in my right ear say, "She is a Prostitute". What? A beautiful lady attending bible school was a prostitute? I found it hard to believe and wondered if I would have an opportunity to confirm it during our meeting. After a few minutes of beating around the bush at the meeting, with my palms sweaty with anxiety at the possibility of being wrong, I plucked up the courage and shared what God had laid on my heart about her. She did not hesitate in confirming it was true. But what if I had never prayed and heard from God about her? Being led of my eyes I could have initiated a relationship with her and she might never have volunteered the information herself. Do not misunderstand me – God loves prostitutes but that information was important for me to know if I was contemplating a relationship with her.

2.   Prophetic Foresight

31 "And the Lord said, "Simon, Simon! Indeed, <u>Satan has asked for you, that he may sift you as wheat.</u>

32 "But I have prayed for you, that your faith should not fail; and when you have returned to Me, strengthen your brethren."

33 But he said to Him, "Lord, I am ready to go with You, both to prison and to death."

34 Then He said, <u>"I tell you, Peter, the rooster shall not crow this day before you will deny three times that you know Me."</u>"- Luke 22:30

This is another dimension of prophetic revelation. It is the ability to perceive future events so as to prepare for it or avert it in prayer. In the case of Simon Peter, the Lord Jesus revealed the events in the scriptures above to Peter so as to reveal his weak areas to him and to get him to prepare to strengthen them in the place of prayer.

I have had numerous incidents of prophetic forewarnings either through dreams, inner promptings or visions. Events in real life then played out as revealed to me in the vision or dream. On one occasion, I was shown in a dream how and where I was going to be betrayed by someone I deemed to be very close to me. This happened exactly as envisaged in the dream 10 months after the actual revelation – it was the same building and group of people as I had seen in the dream.

3. Prophetic Far-sight

The Prophetic does not only pick up things that will happen in 2 weeks, 2 months or 2 years time. It also sees things that will happen in 20 years and perhaps even 2,000 years from the time of revelation. Jesus did not only predict Peter's denial and Judas's betrayal but He also predicted how the gospel would be preached all over the world. He saw from afar off that the gospel would go to remote areas of the world even as far as the place my father's birth on the hills of Ekiti in South West Nigeria, West Africa.

12 " "And because lawlessness will abound, the love of many will grow cold.
13 "But he who endures to the end shall be saved.
14 "And this gospel of the kingdom will be preached in all the world as a witness to all the nations and then the end will come."- Matt24:12-14

Prophets can often see future events. The Old Testament prophets even foresaw the birth, death and resurrection of the Lord Jesus. They even saw the robe he would wear, the city He would be born in, predicted what He would say, how much He would be betrayed for about 3000 years before it happened (Micah 5:2).

I had mentioned earlier that I had a vision about an ostrich with its head in the ground 21 years ago. This revelation only became a physical reality a couple of years (See Chapter 13 for details).

" "But you shall receive power when the Holy Spirit has come upon you; and you shall be witnesses to Me in Jerusalem and in all Judea and Samaria and to the end of the earth." "- Acts1:8

Turn on your Full lights
When talking about Prophetic range and ability the best way to illustrate it is by using the head lights of a car which can only go

as far as about 100 yards, but when the full lights are turned on, the range of view is almost doubled to about 200 yards. An air plane however, has about 3,000 feet range of view. The prophetic sight and ministry can see farther and clearer that most others.

4. Prophetic Hindsight

Prophetic hindsight is the ability to interpret present events in the light of past prophetic revelations. After Peter had denied Jesus by saying "I don't know Him", after the cock had crowed three times, he suddenly realised with prophetic hindsight that this was what Jesus had predicted.

59"Then after about an hour had passed, another confidently affirmed, saying, "Surely this fellow also was with Him, for he is a Galilean."
60 But Peter said, "Man, I do not know what you are saying!" Immediately, while he was still speaking, the rooster crowed.
61 And the Lord turned and looked at Peter. And Peter remembered the word of the Lord, how He had said to him, "Before the rooster crows, you will deny Me three times."
62 So Peter went out and wept bitterly."- Luke 22:59-62

Prophetic hindsight is the ability to give interpretation and glean wisdom from past events for application now or in the future. In the same vein, Peter was able to say that Judas' death had been predicted by David. On the day of Pentecost, Peter by prophetic hindsight, was able to say "This is that which was spoken of by the prophet Joel".

16""Men and brethren, this Scripture had to be fulfilled, which the Holy Spirit spoke before by the mouth of David concerning Judas, who became a guide to those who arrested Jesus;
17 "for he was numbered with us and obtained a part in this ministry."
18 (Now this man purchased a field with the wages of iniquity; and

falling headlong, he burst open in the middle and all his entrails gushed out.

19 And it became known to all those dwelling in Jerusalem; so that field is called in their own language, Akel Dama, that is, Field of Blood.)

20 "For it is written in the book of Psalms: 'Let his dwelling place be desolate and let no one live in it'; and, 'Let another take his office.'"- Acts1:16-20

On the day of Pentecost

Prophets have the uncanny ability to interpret past or present day events and occurrences in the light of past predictive prophecies.

""For these are not drunk, as you suppose, since it is only the third hour of the day.

16 "But this is what was spoken by the prophet Joel:

17 'And it shall come to pass in the last days, says God, That I will pour out of My Spirit on all flesh; Your sons and your daughters shall prophesy, Your young men shall see visions, Your old men shall dream dreams.

18 And on My menservants and on My maidservants I will pour out My Spirit in those days; And they shall prophesy."- Acts 2:15-18

GOD REVEALS HIS SECRETS TO HIS PROPHETS

Do you know that God has Secrets?

"It is the glory of God to conceal a thing: but the honour of kings is to search out a matter."-Prov. 25:2

God chooses to hide some things from us and conceals some things from us until He feels we are prepared or matured enough to handle it responsibly.

""The <u>secret things </u>belong to the LORD our God, but <u>those things</u> <u>which are revealed</u> belong to us and to our children forever, that we may do all the words of this law."
Deut. 29:29

Those who are able to unveil and decode the secret things of God will walk as kings and reign on the high places of this earth.

28""But there is a God in heaven <u>who reveals secrets and</u> He has made known to King Nebuchadnezzar <u>what will be in the latter days</u>. Your <u>dream</u> and the <u>visions</u> of your head upon your bed, were these:
29 "As for you, O king, thoughts came to your mind while on your bed, about what would come to pass after this; and <u>He who reveals</u> <u>secrets has made known to you what will be</u>.
30 "But as for me, this secret has not been revealed to me because I have more wisdom than anyone living, but for our sakes who make known the interpretation to the king and that you may know the thoughts of your heart."- Dan2:28-30

When we are really close enough to Him and trustworthy enough to handle God's secrets responsibly, He will also reveal His own secrets such as the things He plans to do and sometimes, He even reveals other people's secrets to us in order to protect us from, or prepare us before we deal them. He could also choose to do so when he wants us to intervene in their situation.

17"And the LORD said, "Shall I hide <u>from Abraham what I am doing,</u>
18 "since Abraham shall surely become a great and mighty nation and all the nations of the earth shall be blessed in him?"- Gen.18:17, 18

CHAPTER 5

YOU SHOULD BE THE PROPHET OVER YOUR OWN LIFE

LIVING AHEAD OF THE GAME

When one develops prophetic vision it is possible to live ahead of the game i.e. to live with insight into the future before it comes. Instead of being surprised by events and circumstances; the prophetic person would have seen them afar off and is prepared to deal with them – thwarting the plans of the enemy and ensuring that the purposes of God come to pass. So how do we develop prophetic vision? Let's first explore what a vision is, how God envisions (communicates with) people and how we can begin to exercise the prophetic.

What is a Vision?

What God gives to prophets is a vision or a glimpse of the future. A vision is the unfolding of a divine plan or destiny as it relates to an individual. A vision is a divine picture that God and His heavenly hosts and resources will assist in bringing to pass for the individual.

""Before I formed you in the womb I knew you; before you were born I sanctified you; I ordained you a prophet to the nations.""-Jer.1:4

11"But I make known to you, brethren that the gospel which was preached by me is not according to man.
12 For I neither received it from man, nor was I taught it, but it came through the revelation of Jesus Christ...
...15 But when it pleased God, who separated me from my mother's womb and called me through His grace,
16 to reveal His Son in me that I might preach Him among the Gentiles, I did not immediately confer with flesh and blood,"- Gal.1:11-16

Awakening the Prophetic gift

"If there is a prophet among you, I, the LORD, make myself known to him in a vision; I speak to him in a dream."- Num. 12:5, 6

The above scripture makes it clear that one of God's favourite or main ways of introducing Himself (Induction) to potential prophets is in a vision or in a dream (communication). These seem to be the introductory mediums of initiation into the prophetic journey with the Lord; but as the young prophet progresses in his walk, God uses other means and media to speak with him. To the prophetic beginner, He speaks in dreams, but to the mature prophets like Moses He speaks face to face.

7"Not so with My servant Moses; He is faithful in all My house.
8 I speak with him face to face, even plainly and not in dark sayings; and he sees the form of the LORD. Why then were you not afraid to speak against my servant Moses?""
Num. 12:7- 8

Now let's look at the different ways God speaks to people through visions or revelations.

How do you get Vision (Revelation)?
"After these things I looked and behold, a door standing open in heaven. And the first voice which I heard was like a trumpet speaking with me, saying, "Come up here and I will <u>show you things which must take place</u> after this." "- Rev. 4:1

It is important to identify the different ways in which prophetic revelation can come. As you grow in the prophetic, God can speak to you in one of the 12 ways described below. Please remember that one's supernatural experience is never dependent on how spiritual a person is but is dependent on God's sovereignty or the favour he chooses to bestow on an individual.

6"And there are diversities of activities, but it is the same God who works all in all.
7 But the <u>manifestation of the Spirit is given</u> to <u>each one</u> for <u>the profit of all:</u>
8 <u>for to one is given </u>the word of wisdom through the Spirit, to another the word of knowledge through the same Spirit," – 1 Corinth 12:6-8

12 DIMENSIONS OF SUPERNATURAL REVELATION (VISIONARY STATES)
My list of dimensions and types of supernatural revelations and encounters are adapted from James W. Golls list in his book titled, "Discovering the Seer in you.

1.   **Spiritual Perception**
     This means of revelation occurs when a person picks up a signal, impression or direction in his spirit but his mind sees

no visual image. This usually comes in the form of a spiritual nudge, prompt or impression by the Holy Spirit in our spirit.

6"Now when they had gone through Phrygia and the region of Galatia, they were <u>forbidden by the Holy Spirit</u> to preach the word in Asia.
7 After they had come to Mysia, they tried to go into Bithynia, but <u>the Spirit did not permit them.</u> – Acts 16:6-7

2.   Pictorial Vision

This means of revelation is essentially a projection of an image on our inner eye (eye of the heart) or 'mind's eye' by the Holy Spirit of important things concerning people or events while we are fully conscious and awake.

"Then Jesus said to them, "When you lift up the Son of Man, then you will know that I am He and that <u>I do nothing of Myself</u>, but <u>as My Father taught Me, I speak</u> these things… "<u>I speak what I have seen</u> with My Father and you do what you have seen with your father.""-John 8:28, 38

The above scripture shows that Jesus received pictorial images and instructions on what to do and who to heal. This level of supernatural revelation is usually the realm where many who are gifted in words of knowledge operate. Such visions come like flashes of images that are not mentally conjured up and are usually unrelated to what the "Visionary" has seen or heard around them.

My next phase of Prophetic ministry

I had an experience of this kind after concluding my one medical year internship in the city of Ibadan, Nigeria. I began to ask God for directions concerning my next steps in ministry and God revealed the calling and ministry He wanted me to prepare for. While praying on a certain day, He showed me a vision of a bible baked in the form of very sweet bread. I was later told by a colleague that the vision I had reminded him of a scripture in Ezekiel 3:1-3 and I later saw a similar scripture in Revelation 10:7-10.

"Moreover He said to me, "Son of man, <u>eat what you find; eat this scroll</u> and <u>go, speak to the house of Israel."</u>
2 So I opened my mouth and He caused me to eat that scroll.
3 And He said to me, "Son of man, feed your belly and fill your stomach with this scroll that I give you." So I ate and it was <u>in my mouth like honey in sweetness.</u>
with My words to them.
5 "For you are not sent to a people of unfamiliar speech and of hard language, but to the house of Israel"-Ezek3:1-3
"but in the days of the sounding of the seventh angel, when he is about to sound, the mystery of God would be finished, as He declared to His servants the prophets.
8 Then the voice which I heard from heaven spoke to me again and said, "<u>Go, take the little book which is open in the hand of the angel</u> who stands on the sea and on the earth."
9 So I went to the angel and said to him, <u>"Give me the little book."</u> <u>And he said to me, "Take and eat it;</u> and it will make your stomach bitter<u>, but it will be as sweet as honey in your mouth."</u>
10 Then I took the little book out of the angel's hand and ate it and it was as sweet as honey in my mouth. But when I had eaten it, my stomach became bitter."- Rev. 10:7-10

As both these scriptures talk about feeding on the word of God and being sent as a prophet to a people; I could conclude from the vision and scriptures that God was telling me to prepare to operate in the prophetic ministry.

3. **Panoramic Vision**

   'Panorama' according to the Webster dictionary is a picture unrolled before the spectator in such a way as to give an impression of a continuous view. In a panoramic vision, the individual sees a pictorial vision in motion in his mind while awake. One might also hear words in the realm of the spirit.

   "So the Lord said to him, "Arise and go to the street called Straight and inquire at the house of Judas for one called Saul of Tarsus, for behold, he is praying.
   12 "And in a vision he has seen a man named Ananias coming in and putting his hand on him, so that he might receive his sight.""-
   Acts 9:11-12

4. **Audible Visions or Voices**

   15"Now the LORD had told Samuel in his ear the day before Saul came, saying,
   16 "Tomorrow about this time I will send you a man from the land of Benjamin and you shall anoint him commander over My people Israel, that he may save My people from the hand of the Philistines; for I have looked upon My people, because their cry has come to me.""-1 Sam. 9:15-16

   God does sometimes speak with an audible voice. Some individuals have audio visions, which is a picture accompanied with an audible voice. On a few occasions, I have heard a voice in my inner ear as I woke up from sleep, either in the form of a scripture or a phrase, an instruction or direction. When rising from sleep is often a key time for hearing from God as your spirit is most sensitive at this time and gets the least interruptions from your active conscious mind.

5.   **Dream (Night Vision)**

"9 And <u>a vision appeared to Paul in the night.</u> A man of Macedonia stood and pleaded with him, saying, "Come over to Macedonia and help us."
10 Now after he had seen the vision, immediately we sought to go to Macedonia,"
Acts 16:8-10

This form of revelation happens when an individual receives a revelation while dreaming or sleeping. This is the most common medium for revelation and God often speaks to believers and unbelievers alike in this way.

6.   **Trance**

""Now it happened, when I returned to Jerusalem and was praying in the temple, that <u>I was in a trance</u>
18 "and saw Him saying to me, <u>'Make haste and get out of Jerusalem quickly,</u> for <u>they will not receive your testimony concerning Me.'</u> – Acts 22:17

This means of revelation happens when God wants to send a clear, loud and strong message so He suspends ones conscious mind while they are awake in order to give a particular message. Trances are not very common so don't worry if you haven't experienced one. In over 2 decades of being a Christian, I have only had two trances and both occasions where concerning destiny defining issues. God tends to save this method for very special transmissions.

7.   **Angelic Visitation... Acts10:3**

"3 About the ninth hour of the day <u>he saw clearly in a vision an angel of God coming in and saying to him, "Cornelius!"</u>
4 And when he observed him, he was afraid and said, "What is it,

lord?" *So he said to him, "Your prayers and your alms have come up for a memorial before God.*

5 "Now send men to Joppa and send for Simon whose surname is Peter." – Acts 10:3-5

This means of revelation comes as a result of an angelic visitation in which a message from God is given. The word "angel" is mentioned over 190 times in the bible and angelic visitations were commonplace in both the old and new testaments. Again, this form of revelation is not widespread neither is it extinct and some still report frequent angelic visitations.

8.   Divine Visitation

3"As he journeyed he came near Damascus and suddenly <u>a light shone around him from heaven.</u>

4 Then he fell to the ground and <u>heard a voice saying to him, "Saul, Saul, why are you persecuting Me?"</u>

5 And he said, "Who are You, Lord?" Then <u>the Lord said, "I am Jesus, whom you are persecuting. It is hard for you to kick against the goads."</u>

6 So he, trembling and astonished, said, "Lord, what do you want me to do?" Then the Lord said to him, "Arise and go into the city and you will be told what you must do."

7 And the men who journeyed with him stood speechless, hearing a voice but seeing no one." - Acts9:3-7

Divine visitations happen when the Lord himself visits someone to pass on a message in person. This encounter is not experienced through a dream, vision, or an angel but in reality. Moses, Joshua and Gideon are examples of people who had such encounters.

9.   Open Heaven

"Now it came to pass in the thirtieth year, in the fourth month, on the fifth day of the month, as I was among the captives by the River Chebar, <u>that the heavens were opened</u> and <u>I saw visions of God</u>."
- Ezek1:1

When open heavens occurs, it could be accompanied by a revelation in the form of a vision as seen in the case of Ezekiel above or the hearing of an audible voice as in the case of Jesus below. In either case, it ushers the heavenly into the natural realm bringing new understanding of divine issues.

"When all the people were baptized, it came to pass that Jesus also was baptized; and while He prayed, <u>the heaven was opened.</u>
22 And the Holy Spirit descended in bodily form like a dove upon Him and <u>a voice came from heaven which said,</u> "You are My beloved Son; in You I am well pleased.""
Luke 3:21-22

10.   Out of Body experience

"Then <u>the Spirit lifted me up and brought me</u> to the East Gate of the LORD'S house, which faces eastward; and there at the door of the gate were twenty-five men, <u>among whom I saw</u> Jaazaniah the son of Azzur and Pelatiah the son of Benaiah, princes of the people. 2 And He said to me: "Son of man, these are the men who devise iniquity and give wicked counsel in this city," – Ezekiel 11:1-2

This is another rare and uncommon visionary experience in which people are transported to another place without physical movement. Kenneth Hagin Snr. was noted to have had many out of body experiences. Some people have also reported having such experiences when they were very ill or had a near fatal accident in which they saw themselves or their spirit leaving their body behind or rising out of their body. I have had one out of body experience in which my spirit went through a wall while my body remained in a room. God literally took me out of the room I was in to another room in the same house to show me the activities of an individual who had been doing some untoward things. It was a similar experience that Ezekiel had in the scripture above.

11. Translation

39"Now when they came up out of the water, <u>the Spirit of the Lord caught Philip away</u>, so that <u>the eunuch saw him no more;</u> and he went on his way rejoicing.
40 But Philip <u>was found at Azotus.</u> And passing through, he preached in all the cities till he came to Caesarea." – Acts 8:39-40

In this form of revelation, a person is literally translated physically from one place to another i.e. they are moved from one physical location to another (as opposed to an out of body experience in which it is one's spirit that is moving and not one's physical body). This is another uncommon supernatural experience but I do know someone who says he has had this kind of experience.

12. Heavenly Visitation

2"I know a man in Christ who fourteen years ago--whether in the body I do not know, or whether out of the body I do not know, God knows--such a one was caught up to the third heaven.
3 And I know such a man--whether in the body or out of the body I do not know, God knows--
4 how he was caught up into Paradise and heard inexpressible words, which it is not lawful for a man to utter." - 2 Corinth. 12:2-4

This happens when the Spirit of God takes a person up into Heaven on a tour. Some people say they died, visited heaven and were then resurrected from the dead. Some others are taken in the spirit like Paul mentioned in the verses above. Robert Liardon in his book, "I saw heaven" gives a vivid account of his experience of being caught up to heaven at the age of 8.

CHAPTER 6

THE VALUE OF YOUR DREAMS AND VISIONS

UNLOCKING HIDDEN THINGS AND LOCKED DOORS

14"For <u>God may speak</u> in one way, or in another, <u>Yet man does not perceive it.</u>

15 In a <u>dream</u>, in a <u>vision</u> of the night, When deep sleep falls upon men, While slumbering on their beds, 16 Then He <u>opens the ears of men</u> and <u>seals their instruction.</u>

17 In order to turn man from his deed and conceal pride from man,

18 He keeps back his soul from the Pit and his life from perishing by the sword."

Job 33:14-18

Understanding the human complex

Every human being is made up of three parts – the spirit, the soul and the body - each having its different component and particular function for living in the world.

The Function of our Body

As humans, we relate with our physical and material environment through the five senses of our body using our sight, hearing, smell, touch and taste. It is with these bodily senses that we are conscious of the environment around us and as a result respond to external stimuli appropriately. For example, with our body we detect when the weather is cold and look for warm clothing to wear or when we see or hear danger coming we flee in the opposite direction. Through our natural senses, we are able to navigate the natural world properly.

The Function of our Soul

Through our soul, we are conscious of ourselves and other humans and are able to relate with them emotionally and reason logically with them when awake. While asleep, our bodies can respond to touch, cold, or pain without being aware but we can only relate with the world and people around us in our awakened or conscious state through our soul.

The Function of our Spirit

Our spirit is that part of our being that is conscious of God and the spirit or supernatural realm which is very real although it is not visible to the physical eye. Those who argue that the spirit world does not exist because they can't see, hear or touch it with their physical senses are mistaken. The fact that you can not see radio waves or telecommunication signals does not mean that they don't exist; you only need to put on a radio or connect a cell phone to know they exist even though you can't see them.

Likewise, our inability to see the AIDS or swine flu virus does not nullify their existence. One would need a high powered electron microscope to prove their existence but they existed long before you could see them under a microscope. In the same way, God, angels and evil spirits exist but one requires an attuned and sensitive spirit to discern and be aware of their presence.

The acceptance of the reality of the spirit realm and learning to navigate it appropriately is key to operating in the prophetic.

The limitations of Psychics and False Prophets

Psychics, mediums, spiritists, diviners, occultists and witches have access to this realm with their spirit. They are often able to pick up negative movements, waves and signals in the spirit and even access past events and records because their spirit is awake and aware of the spirit realm. However, they are spiritually dead because they are not alive to God and His mind, purposes and plans and therefore the source of their revelation or insight is not God.

> 8"But there is _a spirit in man and_ _the breath of_ the Almighty _gives him_ _understanding._
> 9 _Great men_ are not always wise, nor do _the aged_ always understand justice."
> Job32:8-9

They tend to usually pick up negative things that are about to happen like death, disease, divorce and other disasters because that is the realm Satan works in (the second heavens). They are unable to tap into the realm of God because they have no part in Him and His domain of operations (the third heavens). Psychics tend to see from what you can call an "Evil eye" which can only see into darkness and not into light.

9""if you do not make known the dream to me, there is only one decree for you! For you have agreed to speak lying and corrupt words before me till the time has changed. <u>Therefore tell me the dream</u> and I shall know that you can give me its interpretation."

10 The Chaldeans answered the king and said, "There is <u>not a man on earth who can tell the king's matter;</u> therefore no king, lord, or ruler has ever asked such things of any magician, astrologer, or Chaldean.

11 "It is a difficult thing that the king requests and there is <u>no other who can tell it to the king except the gods, whose dwelling is not with flesh</u>." "- Dan 2:9-11

Don't reveal your secrets to the enemy

There is a realm that Satan, his cohorts and his human agents do not have access to and can only get the information when it is volunteered by a believer himself.

"3 When Herod the king heard this<u>, he was troubled</u> and all Jerusalem with him.

4 And when he had gathered all the chief priests and scribes of the people together<u>, he inquired of them where the Christ was to be born.</u>

5 So they said to him, "<u>In Bethlehem of Judea, for thus it is written by the prophet:</u>

6 'But you, Bethlehem, in the land of Judah, Are not the least among the rulers of Judah; For out of you shall come a Ruler Who will shepherd My people Israel.'"

7 Then Herod, when he <u>had secretly called the wise men,</u> determined from them <u>what time the star appeared</u>…. 12 Then, being <u>divinely warned in a dream</u> that they should not return to Herod, they departed for their own country another way.

13 Now when they had departed, behold, <u>an angel of the Lord appeared to Joseph in a dream,</u> saying, "Arise, take the young Child and His mother, flee to Egypt and stay there until I bring you word; for <u>Herod</u>

will seek the young Child to destroy Him."

14 When he arose, he took the young Child and His mother by night and departed for Egypt,

15 and <u>was there until the death of Herod</u>, that it might be fulfilled which was spoken by the Lord through the prophet, saying, "Out of Egypt I called My Son." "- Matt. 2:3-15

What are Dreams and Visions?

When we are asleep, our body is at rest and our soul is turned inward (awareness or consciousness of the world around us is shut down) while our spirit is very much alive and active and communes with God and the spirit world.

14"For <u>God may speak</u> in one way, or in another, <u>Yet man does not perceive it.</u>

15 In a <u>dream</u>, in a <u>vision</u> of the night, When deep sleep falls upon men, While slumbering on their beds, 16 Then He <u>opens the ears of men</u> and <u>seals their instruction.</u> Job 33:14-16 "-

According to Rev. Joe Olaiya in his book, "Winning the battles of life",

A <u>dream</u> is the consciousness of activity that engages the spirit and soul realm which takes place while the body is asleep.

A v<u>ision</u> is a consciousness of activity that engages the spirit and soul realm and it takes place while the body is awake'.

In both cases, messages can be received with the "antenna" of the spirit man in the form of spiritual signals, which can then be relayed as pictures or sound which is received, appreciated and is perceived in our soul. This system operates in a similar way to how a television operates where invisible waves are received but are then relayed in pictorial form on a TV screen. Signals from the spirit realm are relayed as a pictorial sequence on the screen of our soul.

With the aid of dreams, man is able to perceive present spiritual realities, preview events in the future or take a peak into past events by the revelation of the Spirit.

In most dreams and visions when you suddenly re-unite with your bodily senses you have a vivid impression of the events which are often stored in your memory. In the dream state, the soul is still very much alive in its functions of consciousness, memory, reasoning and feeling but at the level of the sub-conscious state without the engagement of the world around it. This is why dreams should be recalled, processed, relayed or written down when one wakes up in order to capture the message therein.

"…When <u>deep sleep</u> falls upon men, While slumbering on their beds, 16 Then He (God) <u>opens the ears of men</u> and <u>seals their instruction…</u>"- Job 33:14-16

Some scientific observations concerning dreams by Mark and Patti Vickler

Sleep laboratories have proven that everyone dreams one to two hours each night during a certain period of sleep known as alpha level, which is light sleep. Every 90-minute cycle of sleep begins with alpha and then goes into deeper sleep which is called theta and finally deepest sleep which is called delta. At the close of the first 90-minute cycle each night, the individual returns to alpha level sleep, where he has a short, five-minute dream period. The next time he cycles up to alpha, he has a ten-minute dream period. The third time in alpha, the dream period is about 15 minutes and so on. If one sleeps a full eight hours, the entire last hour is essentially spent in alpha level sleep. Thus, the average person sleeping for eight hours a night will dream about one to two hours of that time. Alpha level sleep is where one has what is called Rapid Eye Movement (REM). Rapid Eye Movement is exactly what it sounds like: the eyes of the dreamer begin moving rapidly. He is actually watching the scenes in the dream and thus his eyes are literally moving back and forth, observing the action. By observing the alpha level sleep when Rapid Eye Movement occurs, researchers in sleep laboratories have determined when a person is dreaming and how much time is spent dreaming on an average night.

The Sources of Dreams
There are four main sources of dreams
1.   God
2.   Devil
3.   Self
4.   Other Sources - i.e. dreams induced by
     i.   Physiology i.e. natural processes
     ii.   Biochemical e.g. drugs, alcohol , food, fever, pregnancy,
     iii.   Seductions i.e. interactions with someone seductive
     iv.   False dreams e.g. Jer. 23:18-26

We will look at the dreams that are inspired by God for the rest of this chapter.

Different types of Dreams
God gives us dream messages (or messages through dreams) for different reasons and at different seasons in our lives. God is so kind and loving that he gave Jesus' father, Joseph many directions concerning his bride-to-be, impending danger and

places to live at various times so as to be safe.

The different kind of dream messages God sends are discussed below.

1. **Direction dreams**
    This kind of dream is one in which God gives specific directions to the dreamer. An example is found in Acts16:6-10.

    6"Now when they had gone through Phrygia and the region of Galatia, <u>they were forbidden by the Holy Spirit to preach the word in Asia.</u>
    7 After they had come to Mysia, they tried to go into Bithynia, <u>but the Spirit did not permit them.</u>
    8 So passing by Mysia, they came down to Troas.
    9 <u>And a vision appeared to Paul in the night</u>. A <u>man of Macedonia stood and pleaded with him, saying, "Come over to Macedonia and help us."</u>
    10 Now after he had seen the vision, immediately we sought to go to Macedonia, concluding that the Lord had called us to preach the gospel to them."- Acts16:6-10

    The above passage shows that God did not let Paul go into Asia when he tried to do so on a couple of occasions but instead gave him clear directions in a dream (night vision) to go to Macedonia instead. God is also able to give us prophetic direction concerning what to do and where to go if we seek His guidance. When I was contemplating if I should write my fifth book titled "12 things you don't know that could be destroying you", I was very hesitant about going ahead with it, because I was aware it is a book that exposes the enemy's subtle and hidden activities in peoples lives and I knew it could provoke some spiritual warfare. I was sitting on the edge of my bed on a certain day with some hesitation in my heart as to whether I should start writing the book when I received a text about a dream from a member of my church which indicated that it was time to start writing it albeit it with extensive spiritual and prayer covering.

2. **Instruction dreams**

These dreams come to give us wisdom as to how to do things. If direction dreams tell us "what to do", instruction dreams tell us "how to do it". Within the first few years of starting my publishing business, I noticed we were always in the red financially and that we were continuously operating out of our bank overdraft. This was a challenging period even though we were getting good jobs and our client base was growing and so I began praying to God concerning the situation.

Shortly after praying about the business situation, I had a dream in which I saw Robert Kiyosaki (a business teacher and financial mentor) and a diagram of quadrants showing "hands" in some of the quadrants and "mouths on heads" in the others. I looked closely and noticed that there were about 4 mouths to 2 hands in the diagram. When I woke up, it immediately dawned on me that this was an instructional dream about my business overheads. The dream was saying that there was an imbalance in my business - that there were more "mouths on heads" to feed than "hands" bringing in income and that was why the business was literally living from "hand to mouth". As a result, I was able to reassess the business and noted that we had taken on more staff than we could manage at the time as well as office space and rent overheads that we were not quite ready for. In this dream, God was able to give me an accurate picture of what the cause of the problem was in my business so that I could deduce what to do.

3.   **Exposure e.g. Secret Sins, Demonic roots**
Sometimes, dreams come to reveal something that is hidden that we need to know or address. I have had numerous dreams in which God reveals people's past or present sins.

I have had dreams in which God showed me someone who was having a secret sexual affair, someone who had had an abortion and someone stealing and manipulating records. Each individual confirmed what had been revealed in the dream when I confronted them as it was clear to them that only God could have revealed the facts to me. Exposure dreams usually come after God has given many warnings to a person without him or her taking the heed.

Adulterer's phone number revealed
A certain lady had a dream in which a particular phone number was revealed to her. On waking up, she had no idea who the number belonged to but she wrote it down on a piece of paper. She then stored the number on her phone contacts under the title "Who". A few weeks later her phone rang and the title that showed up on her phone was 'Who'. She picked up the phone and it was the number of a lady at her church who she had previously counselled and mentored. She later found out that her husband had being having an affair with the lady. Why on earth was that number revealed to her if it was not to point out that she

needed to be mindful of the person with that number? God was clearly telling her by revealing that number to her that she needed to know something about the person whose number that was. God is a revealer of secrets.

4. **Correction dreams**

At times, dreams are given to us to correct us or instruct us to change certain things. After I had just finished preaching one Sunday morning, a young man walked up to tell me that he had a dream the night before in which he heard his father's voice as he was walking towards a sewage pit. He approached me because in the message I gave an illustration of how God would love and embrace us despite our sin, just like a father would still embrace his son who fell into a sewage pit. My illustration was to show that no matter how filthy we are when we fall into sin, the Father still loves us and desires to draw us close. The conclusion we came to was that God, through his dream and my Sunday message, was trying to correct him and teach him not to wilfully walk into sin.

There is a biblical example of this in Genesis 20:1-7.

1"And Abraham journeyed from there to the South and dwelt between Kadesh and Shur and stayed in Gerar.

2 Now Abraham said of Sarah his wife, "She is my sister." And Abimelech king of Gerar sent and took Sarah.

3 But <u>God came to Abimelech in a dream by night</u> and said to him, "<u>Indeed you are a dead man because of the woman whom you have taken, for she is a man's wife.</u>"

4 But Abimelech had not come near her; and he said, "Lord, will You slay a righteous nation also?

5 "Did he not say to me, 'She is my sister'? And she, even she herself said, 'He is my brother.' In the integrity of my heart and

innocence of my hands I have done this."
6 And God said to him in a dream, "Yes, I know that you did this
in the integrity of your heart. For I also withheld you from sinning
against Me; therefore I did not let you touch her.
7 "Now therefore, restore the man's wife; for he is a prophet and
he will pray for you and you shall live. But if you do not restore
her, know that you shall surely die, you and all who are yours." "-
Genesis 20:1-7.

We can see in this example that God showed up to
Abimelech in a dream to warn him of committing a grave
sin. Albeit, one he would have committed unknowingly.
God did this to prevent Abimelech and his family from a
severe punishment and to preserve Sarah's integrity and
purity as a married woman.

5.   Warning dreams
This kind of dream comes when God is trying to warn us
concerning impending danger. He informs us ahead about
dangerous situations and dangerous people around us and
also of people who are in danger.

"Then, being divinely warned in a dream that they should not
return to Herod, they departed for their own country another way.
Now when they had departed, behold, an angel of the Lord
appeared to Joseph in a dream, saying, "Arise, take the young
Child and His mother, flee to Egypt and stay there until I bring
you word; for Herod will seek the young Child to destroy Him." "-
Matt. 2:12,13

God has revealed to me various temptations and traps He
wanted me to avoid in advance of the event. Once, I had a
dream where I saw my two sons lying down on the floor

and playing in the jungle when suddenly the older one got up and started running while the younger one was still lying down. When my older son eventually looked back, he noticed a lion at my younger son heels and it was too late to rescue him. When I woke up, I realised I had to pray against some impending attack on my son's life. A week later, my younger son was diagnosed with the potentially lethal swine flu disease virus which was killing young children at the time but my older son escaped catching the infection. I believe because I had prepared in prayer, the infection was mild and he recovered swiftly. Many diseases and tragedies have their root cause in the spiritual realm and need to be prayed about before they manifest in the physical tangible realm. That is why God gives warning dreams.

6. **Deliverance or Healing dreams**
    Sometimes, God gives dreams to confirm victory in an area. I refer to such dreams as 'deliverance dreams'. They come to show the emancipation of the subject from bondage, liberation from a curse, breaking of a soul tie, healing or cleansing of a wound.
    In such a dream, the individual may be seen escaping from prison or prison guards or breaking free from chains. These sorts of dream usually occur after a season of prayer and or fasting or after a deliverance prayer session.

7. **Ordination or Impartation dreams**
    These kinds of dreams happen when God anoints or ordains a person for a particular mission or assignment. An example of this is found in 1Kings 3:5-15.

    5"At Gibeon <u>the LORD appeared to Solomon in a dream by night;</u> and God said, <u>"Ask! What shall I give you?"</u>

6 And Solomon said: "You have shown great mercy to Your servant David my father, because he walked before You in truth, in righteousness and in uprightness of heart with You; You have continued this great kindness for him and You have given him a son to sit on his throne, as it is this day.

7 "Now, O LORD my God, You have made Your servant king instead of my father David, but I am a little child; I do not know how to go out or come in.

8 "And Your servant is in the midst of Your people whom You have chosen, a great people, too numerous to be numbered or counted.

9 "Therefore give to Your servant an understanding heart to judge Your people, that I may discern between good and evil. For who is able to judge this great people of Yours?"

10 The speech pleased the Lord, that Solomon had asked this thing.

11 Then God said to him: "Because you have asked this thing and have not asked long life for yourself, nor have asked riches for yourself, nor have asked the life of your enemies, but have asked for yourself understanding to discern justice,

12 "behold, I have done according to your words; see, I have given you a wise and understanding heart, so that there has not been anyone like you before you, nor shall any like you arise after you.

13 "And I have also given you what you have not asked: both riches and honor, so that there shall not be anyone like you among the kings all your days.

14 "So if you walk in My ways, to keep My statutes and My commandments, as your father David walked, then I will lengthen your days."

15 Then Solomon awoke; and indeed it had been a dream. And he came to Jerusalem and stood before the ark of the covenant of the LORD, offered up burnt offerings,"

1 Kings 3:5-15.

God responded to Solomon's extravagant sacrifice by asking him what he wanted in a dream. He then imparted the spirit of wisdom, riches and honour to him in his dream.

Joan of Arc became a national heroine of France in the 1400s. She was a peasant girl born in Eastern France who through a dream was ordained and anointed by God to lead the French army into several victories during the hundred years' war, which paved the way for Charles VII.

8.   **Innovation dreams**
Scientists like Benzene, Einstein, and Bohr are reported to have gotten some of their scientific breakthroughs in their dreams. Benzene is an aromatic resin used by pharmacists and perfumers which is signified by the chemical symbol of a hexagon. The chemist who discovered and designed the hexagon as its symbol was said to have gotten the inspiration for the hexagon from seeing a snake with its tail in its mouth in his dream.

About 10 years ago, I met a very successful business woman who owned several hair dressing salons across the U.K. She mentioned that she had received the vision for her business in a dream.

9.   **Comforting dreams**
God sometimes gives individual dreams to allay their fears or comfort them in times of crisis. Paul was comforted or encouraged in the book of Acts in a dream on two different recorded occasions. One of them was when the ship he was sailing in was caught in a fierce storm and the second time was when he arrived at a certain city after almost being killed in a previous city. These were two very traumatic

events and God recognised that he needed reassurance at these times.

22""And now <u>I urge you to take heart,</u> for <u>there will be no loss of life among you,</u> but only of the ship.
23 "For <u>there stood by me this night an angel of the God</u> to whom I belong and whom I serve,
24 "saying, 'Do not be afraid, Paul; you must be brought before Caesar;<u> and indeed God has granted you all those who sail with you.</u>'
25 "Therefore take heart, men, for I believe God that it will be just
26 "However, we must run aground on a certain island." – Acts 27:22-26
"Now <u>the Lord spoke to Paul in the night by a vision,</u> "<u>Do not be afraid, but speak and do not keep silent;</u>
10 "for <u>I am with you and</u> <u>no one will attack you to hurt you;</u> for I have many people in this city."
11 And he continued there a year and six months, teaching the word of God among them." Acts18:9-11

10. Confirmation dreams

These dreams are usually given by God to the individual in question or someone else to confirm what God has already told the individual. We see this played out when was God recruiting Gideon in Judges 7:13-15.

13"And when Gideon had come, <u>there was a man telling a dream to his companion</u>. He said, "<u>I have had a dream:</u> To my surprise, a loaf of barley bread tumbled into the camp of Midian; it came to a tent and struck it so that it fell and overturned and the tent collapsed."
14 Then his companion answered and said, "<u>This is nothing else</u>

but the sword of Gideon the son of Joash, a man of Israel! Into his
hand God has delivered Midian and the whole camp."
15 And so it was, when Gideon heard the telling of the dream and
its interpretation, that he worshiped. He returned to the camp of
Israel and said, "Arise, for the LORD has delivered the camp of
Midian into your hand."" – Judges 7:13-15

God gave Gideon's enemies confirmation of what He had
already told Gideon – that he would overpower them.

11. Preparation or Promotion dreams
This is the kind of dream where God reveals what he is about
to do with a person so that the individual can prepare in
advance for the assignment. God encouraged Jeremiah in this
way in *Jeremiah 1:17-19*.

""Therefore prepare yourself and arise and speak to them all that I
command you. Do not be dismayed before their faces, Lest I dismay
you before them.
18 For behold, I have made you this day A fortified city and an iron
pillar and bronze walls against the whole land-Against the kings of
Judah, Against its princes, Against its priests and against the people
of the land.
19 They will fight against you, But they shall not prevail against
you. For I am with you," says the LORD, "to deliver you."" –
Jeremiah 1:17-19

This brings to mind a certain dream that a minister at the
church I pastor had. In the dream, he was called by a certain
notable figure with whom he had had no previous personal
dealings to help out in a media venture. At the time, he was
working for a bank. About 5 years later, he was indeed called
to manage a TV station spearheaded by this individual.

12. **Spiritual Warfare dreams**
    Demonic assignments in dreams
    Satan and his cohorts attack in the spiritual realm before it manifests in the natural realm and God can reveal the plot to us in the spiritual realm where it is being conceived before it manifests in the physical realm. This is so that we can be aware and avert the enemy's plans by uprooting whatever has been planted and destroying whatever edifice the enemy might be erecting. I have had dreams where I was attacked in a dream and later the same thing played out itself in the material world. I had a dream once where I saw an old female friend who had not made contact with me in 11 years trying to seduce me. The next day I got a phone call out of the blue saying she was in town. Needless to say, I wasn't in a rush to meet up with her.

13. **Defeat in Dreams**
    Sometimes, individuals dream that they were defeated in a dream. This usually happens because a door was opened or the individual does not have enough strength at the time to deal with what is coming up against him or her. Such a dream may also be indicating that s/he is being outnumbered because s/he doesn't have enough spiritual or prayer covering i.e. that the individual is spiritually vulnerable.

    I once had a dream in which I saw about 6 watchmen guarding my home one night and I went out to check if they were alright. I noticed they were huddled together conversing rather than standing watch on the perimeter of my property. I then noticed about 60 armed men dressed in black who then climbed through the hedge on the perimeter of my property and handcuffed me and the watchmen and took us and members of my family and congregation captive. A certain intercessor in Nigeria had picked up by revelation that a certain demonic onslaught had been conceived against me and he advised me to raise intercessors to pray for me and my ministry. A few months after the dream, I experienced a sustained attack on myself, my family and ministry for an extended period. We overcame it by sustained prayer personally and through a group of intercessors that we raised up.

14. Victory in Dreams
Victory in warfare dreams usually comes after a time of repentance, deliverance or after building oneself up through a season of prayer and fasting.

A friend of mine told me a fascinating story about an experience that her husband had a couple of years ago. In a dream, he saw some huge (Samurai like) warriors in a fierce armed combat and one of them had started heading towards him with a raised sword when he woke up from his sleep. His wife mentioned that she had noticed he was sweating and trembling just before he woke up. The next day, they decided to pray against the enemy's plans as revealed in the dream. While they were praying, he suddenly slumped back and he fell into a trance. She tried to wake him up but couldn't and fear started to build as she thought he might have died.

Approximately 15 minutes later, he awoke and said he had a vision in which he was taken to the exact point where he had left off in the dream the night before and that this time he lifted up his sword and cut off the head of the warrior like figure. This gentleman is the first grandson of a certain late but very notable figure in Nigeria who is noted as one of the spearheads and founders of one of the main mystical fraternities in Nigeria. A few days following the incident, they heard that his cousin who was the next oldest grandson had suddenly died. He had no previous history of illness. My friend and her husband believe that he was the one meant to die but when they dealt with it in prayer, the baton was passed on to the next grandson who was unprepared to deal with it.

Whenever we experience defeats or oppressive attacks in a dream, we should always ensure that we fortify ourselves spiritually and rise up and make declarations to cancel the enemy's plans before they hatch.

I hope in this chapter, you have come to recognise that your dreams are very important and a key way to enter the prophetic. God wants to direct, instruct, correct, warn and protect you through your dreams. Take them seriously. Get a notebook, keep it by your bedside and get into the habit of noting down details of the dreams you have as soon as you wake up. In so doing you will be developing an arsenal of protection.

CHAPTER 7

INTERPRETING YOUR DREAMS AND VISIONS

There are certain guiding principles, rules and methodology we can apply to the interpretation of our dreams and visions in order to decode or unlock God's message to us.

These guidelines and principles are outlined and discussed below.

How to interpret visions & Dreams
A. Observation
What do you see?

B. Interpretation
What do you think it means?

C. Application
What does it mean to us today i.e. what should we do in response?

Medium of interpreting dreams
i. Soul - by Reasoning - Acts10:17
ii. Spirit - by Revelation - Acts10:19

The Medium of Reasoning:

A Mental Framework for interpreting dreams
i. Context
Are you a Participator or an Observer in the dream?
Is the dream about you or someone else?
Is it in Colour or Black and White?
Where is the dream taking place? Is it in your house (present or past), the church, in a classroom etc.

ii. Compartments
Is the dream in one single part or is it in sections or compartments that can be divided into chapters?
Are the parts progressing or regressing?

iii. Characters
Who is the main character in the dream? You or someone else
Who are the other characters and what do they represent?

iv. Content
What is the storyline of the dream?
What were your feelings within the dream?
What are your emotions on waking up from the dream?

v. Components
What are the various elements within the dream? The key symbols, numbers, colours, animals, vehicles and dates etc.

Other guidelines for Dream interpretation
a. Most dreams are symbolic and not literal. A dream is like a caricature or an exaggeration to emphasise a point.

b. What did the dream mean to you the dreamer in particular?

c. Interpret out of the repertoire of your understanding before you begin to make use of common dream symbols

d. Who is the main character?

e. When you observe a person in a dream, what is their dominant trait, what do they represent to you or what is the meaning of their name?

f. Take note of how you feel in the dream

g. Recurrent dreams over time are usually a repetition for emphasis and an indication that the person has not understood, heeded or obeyed the recurrent instruction yet.

h. Successive dreams in the same night are usually dealing with the same issue but looking at it from different angles

i. Successive dreams in the same night could also mean the dream is confirmed or certain and soon to happen

1*"In the first year of Belshazzar king of Babylon, Daniel had a dream and visions of his head while on his bed. Then he wrote down the dream,* *telling <u>the main facts</u>.*

2 Daniel spoke, saying, "I saw in my vision by night and behold, the four winds of heaven were stirring up the Great Sea."- Dan. 7:1-2

22 "And he informed me and talked with me and said, "O Daniel, I have now come forth to <u>give you skill to understand.</u>

23 "At the beginning of your supplications the command went out and I have come to tell you, for you are greatly beloved; therefore <u>consider the matter and <u>understand the vision:</u></u>"-Dan9:22-23

CHAPTER 8

UNDERSTANDING THE LANGUAGE OF GOD

PICTURES AND SYMBOLS

The use of Pictures and Symbols

When God speaks to us, He doesn't always communicate in words as we do. Instead, He usually uses imagery in communicating with us i.e. pictures, stories and symbols.

Why does God choose to use pictures?

A picture speaks louder than a thousand words. One picture can be worth a thousand words and many parables are basically illustrations or pictures in motion. The passages below show God uses the natural things He created to become symbols which are used to unveil or explain spiritual truths. All truths we are told are parallel or universal.

19"Because what may be known of God is manifest in them, for God has shown it to them.

20 For since the creation of the world His <u>invisible attributes</u> are <u>clearly</u> <u>seen</u>, being <u>understood</u> by the <u>things that are made</u>, even His eternal power and Godhead, so that they are without excuse,"-
Romans 1:19- 20

46"However, the <u>spiritual</u> is not first, but the <u>natural and</u> afterward the spiritual.
47 <u>The first man</u> was <u>of the earth</u>, made of dust; <u>the second Man</u> is the <u>Lord from heaven</u>."-1Corinthans 15:46-47

God speaks mostly in Parables
Even when God does speak He tends to do so in parables.

Old Testament
6"Then He said, "Hear now My words: If there is a prophet among you, I, the LORD, make Myself known to him in a vision; I speak to him in a dream.
7 Not so with my servant Moses; He is faithful in all my house.
8 I speak with him face to face, even plainly and not in <u>dark sayings</u> <u>(parables);</u> and he sees the form of the LORD. Why then were you not afraid to speak against my servant Moses?" "- Numbers12:6-8

New Testament
10"But when He was alone, those around Him with the twelve asked Him about the parable.
11 And He said to them, "<u>To you it has been given to know the mystery</u> of the kingdom of God; but <u>to those who are outside, all things come in</u> <u>parables,</u>
12 "so that 'seeing they may see and <u>not perceive</u> and hearing they may hear and <u>not understand;</u> lest they should turn and their sins be forgiven them.'"
13 And He said to them, "Do you not understand this parable? How then will you understand all the parables?"- Mark 4:10-13

Why does God use Parables when speaking to us?

1. To conceal things from others and keep them in the dark (dark sayings).

    God wants to keep things from some people so He has His own code that He uses which only the initiated can decode.

2. So that we can search out the meaning and depend on Him for the interpretation.

    God wants us to lean on Him and learn from Him. This often only happens when things are too difficult for us to figure out by ourselves.

3. One parable can also carry multi-dimensional messages and could speak to different people in different ways.

    In this way, God is not limited or boxed in but is able to minister to a variety of people or in a variety of ways using the same parable.

4. The element of time release and sensitivity.

    This means that portions of the parable become clearer with time as we ponder it, giving the full meaning time to unfold.

5. To create a sense of exclusivity.

    God is on another realm and is mysterious. The use of parables maintains a sense of awe and wonder at His wisdom.

What is a Parable?

The word Parable literally means to "throw along side".

According to Dictionary.com

- It is a short allegorical story designed to illustrate or teach some truth, religious principle or moral lesson.
- It is a statement or comment that conveys a meaning indirectly

by the use of comparison, analogy or the like.

According to the "Dictionary of Biblical imagery" by Leland Ryken et al, the Parables of Jesus can be put under two major headings 'Realism' and 'Symbolism'.

A. Realism

This type of parable is a simple story that portrays life as we find it in the world e.g. parables using farming, fishing, trading or baking illustrations. Jesus uses common secular practices to explain deep spiritual truths that have profound spiritual meaning and significance in order to capture the mind and arrest the understanding of the everyday man. Examples of this are the parable of the sower which is about a farmer sowing seeds used to illustrate the sowing of spiritual seeds; the parable of talents which uses the management of money to illustrate the use of resources entrusted to each individual and the parable of the lost coin which uses the story of a woman's search for a lost coin to illustrate God's seeking after lost souls.

In the same vein, Paul also uses a lot of parables to communicate spiritual principles to his audience. In a case where he was trying to communicate the principle of blessing spiritual tutors he says,

6"Or is it only Barnabas and I who have no <u>right to refrain from working?</u>
7 Who (Soldier) ever <u>goes to war at his own expense</u>? Who (Farmer) <u>plants a vineyard and does not eat of its fruit</u>? Or who (Shepherd) tends a flock and does not drink of the milk of the flock?
8 Do I say these things as a mere man? Or does not the law say the same also?
9 for it is written in the law of Moses, "You shall not <u>muzzle an ox</u>

while it treads out the grain." Is it oxen God is concerned about?
10 Or does He say it altogether for our sakes? For our sakes, no doubt,
this is written, that he who plows should plow in hope and he who
threshes in hope should be partaker of his hope.
11 If we have sown spiritual things for you, is it a great thing if we reap
your material things?"- 1Corinthians 9:6-11

B. Symbolism

Symbolism is the practice of representing things by symbols, or investing things with a symbolic meaning or character. In these parables, Jesus made it clear that the story was not literal and that it had a second deeper meaning than it is first perceived. In these sorts of parables, He would usually start with words such as *"The Kingdom of Heaven is like…"* In order to make it clear that he was using an earthly picture to try to describe a heavenly reality (Mark 4:26).

THE KEYS TO UNLOCKING THE MYSTERY IN OUR DREAMS

A.   Understanding by Keys of Symbolic language

10"But when He was alone, those around Him with the twelve asked
Him about the parable.
11 And He said to them, "To you it has been given to know the
mystery of the kingdom of God; but to those who are outside, all
things come in parables,… The sower sows the word (Seed).
15 "And these are the ones by the wayside where the word is sown.
When they hear, Satan (birds of the air) comes immediately and takes
away the word that was sown in their hearts.

16 "These likewise are the ones sown on stony ground who, when they hear the word, immediately receive it with gladness;.... "- Mark 4:11-18

To fully interpret and understand the meaning of a parable, you need the key or meaning to each symbol contained therein. The keys can usually be deduced from things around the dreamer or interpreter that are accessible and are readily understandable. God is not trying to hide things from us but desires to release information to us at the appointed time. See below for some illustrations of this.

1. **Nature**
   The Four seasons: Spring, Summer, Autumn and Winter
   What each season represents can be deduced from the key characteristic of that season.

   Spring means: Time of Growth – plants and flowers are budding in nature at this time.
   Summer means: Time of Fruitfulness – fruits ripen at this time in nature.
   Autumn means: Time of Decline – flowers begin to fall off as the weather grows cold.
   Winter means: Time of Loss or Hibernation – as the cold weather sets in, flowers die and much of nature hibernates or withdraws.

2. **Scripture**
   Symbols in Scripture – Seed, Field, Birds, Weed, Locust,
   Some symbols take their meaning or significance from how they are used in scripture (Mark 4:1-20).
   Seed means the Word of God because the scripture uses seed as an example of the word.

Birds mean Satan and his demons because the scripture uses birds as an example of the devourer.

Weed means distractions i.e. care of this world, deceitfulness of riches because the scripture uses weeds as an example of the distractions.

Locust means curses, punishment or judgement because the scripture uses locust as an example of the curses.

3. **Culture**
    The cultural significance of a symbol can also be a key indicator of the meaning of a picture. For example Big Ben represents the seat of political power in England or precision in timing and measurement. The meaning to be given to it will depend on the context of the dream. Making a "V" sign with ones index and middle finger could mean victory in one culture and profanity and an insult in another - again the context in which it is used is very important.

    A good example of cultural relevance in interpretation is coming out of water. In the Christian environment in the Western world, it could mean a person is coming into resurrection as in a water baptism experience. However, in an African context and depending on the surrounding factors in the dream, it could signify a connection to the under world or ancestral links with a water or marine spirit.

4. **Common Language**
    - Proverbs, metaphors, simile, word plays
    Before we talk about the symbolic meaning of these, let us have a quick look at the meaning of each word.

Metaphor
A metaphor is a figure of speech in which a term or phrase is

applied to something to which it is not literally applicable in order to suggest a resemblance, as in *"A mighty fortress is our God."*

Simile

A simile is a common figure of speech that explicitly compares two things which are usually considered different. Most similes are introduced by *like* or *as: "The realization hit me like a bucket of cold water."*

Proverb

A proverb is a short popular saying which effectively expresses some commonplace truth or useful thought e.g. *"You can't teach an old dog new tricks"*

This is another set of interpretation like the last, in which the cultural significance or meaning of the proverb or metaphor for example, is important in understanding it.

Phrases such as "Like a fish out of water" or "An ostrich with its head in the sand" should be given the ordinary cultural meaning.

Personal Expressions (Internal Jokes)

These are certain experiences and expressions that may be common to a few like a family or church or just to the individual in question. These should usually be taken to have the meaning they have to you.

Understanding by the Key of the Spirit

Many times, we can unravel our dreams ourselves with the help of the Holy Spirit. As we ponder upon the revelation, the Spirit of God will aid our understanding and give us the interpretation Himself.

> *19 "While Peter <u>thought about the vision</u>, the Spirit said to him, "Behold, three men are seeking you.*
> *20 "Arise therefore, go down and go with them, doubting nothing; for I have sent them." "*
> *Acts 10:19-20*

Understanding by the Key of a Guide

At other times, God may send or require us to go to a skilled or gifted interpreter to help us interpret our dreams or visions.

> *29 "Then <u>the Spirit said to Philip</u>, "Go near and overtake this chariot."*
> *30 So Philip ran to him and heard him reading the prophet Isaiah and said, <u>"Do you understand what you are reading?"</u>*
> *31 And he said, "<u>How can I, unless someone guides me?</u>" And he asked Philip to come up and sit with him."- Acts8:29-31*

This guide can be a pastor, prophet or someone who is skilled in dream interpretation with a proven track record. You can often access such a person's wisdom by the use of Christian dream dictionaries and books. I have found such books invaluable in providing knowledge on key areas such as the significance of numbers, colours and such like which are biblically based. I share some of this below.

Some other Significant Keys to Dream interpretation

Significant Numbers

Numbers e.g. 1, 2, 3, 4, 5, 6, 7, 8, 9, 10, 11, 12, 30, 40, 60, 100
5 is the Number of grace, 7 is the Number of Perfection, 10 is the Number of Measurement, 12 is the Number of Government, 40 is the Number of Testing and 100 Number of Full measure or Reward.

Significant Colours

Colours e.g. Red, Blue, Green, Purple, Gold, Silver, Bronze

Red is the Colour of Redemption, Blue is the Colour of the Spiritual or Prophetic, Purple represents Royalty, Gold speaks of Divinity and Bronze Suffering.

Significant People

People e.g. Friend, Stranger, Pastor, Teacher and Grandparent

A Friend may sometimes represent you or the Holy Spirit in a dream, a good Stranger might signify an Angel and a bad Stranger could represent a Demon, a Pastor may represent Spiritual authority or God Himself in a dream and a Grandparent may signify Ancestral or inherited things.

Significant Places

Buildings e.g. House, Living room, Bedroom, Basement, Bathroom

Your House could mean anything from the individual's life to his family or the church, Living room signifies revealed things, Bedroom speaks of intimate things, Basement signifies hidden or secret things and Bathroom either speaks of Lust or Repentance or Cleansing.

Significant Animals

Animals e.g. Lion, Eagle, Dove, Ox

A Lion could signify the Lord Jesus, Dominion, or even the devil, an Eagle could represent Leadership or the Prophet, a Dove the Holy Spirit and an Ox could speak of Work, Ministry or Increase or Prosperity.

Significant Directions

Direction e.g. Front, Back, Right, Left, North, East, West, South

Front usually speaks of the Future, Back the Past, Right represents the Natural realm, Left represents the Spiritual realm, North represents where God dwells.

Significant Vehicles

Vehicles e.g. Car, Bus, Plane, Ship

A Car usually speaks of an individual's life, Destiny or Ministry, a Van may represent a Family, Bus signifies a Ministry, an Airplane usually represents a Prophetic ministry and Warship may signify Prayer warfare.

CHAPTER 9

10 WAYS TO KNOW WHEN GOD IS SPEAKING

I believe it is important to know and understand that God does speak in different ways. I have mainly emphasised and elaborated on the medium of dreams because I believe it is the most universal of all the media that God can use. It is universal because every human being regardless of colour, class, or creed has had a dream at one time in their life or another.

In the Bible, God spoke to the heathen wicked kings through the medium of dreams. He spoke to Nebuchadnezzar, Pharaoh, Abimelech and even the Wife of Pontius Pilate. It is however important to note that God speaks to His children in different ways.

Hearing from God is the most important thing in our Christian walk. Everything we do in Christianity is premised on our ability to hear God e.g. what job to do, whom to marry, what church to join, where to live.

"And the sheep follow him, for they know his voice."-John 10:4

"The LORD is my Shepherd; I shall not want. He makes me to lie down in green pastures; He leads me beside the still waters. He restores my soul; He leads me in the paths of righteousness". - Psalm 23:1-3

"For as many as are led by the Spirit of God, these are sons of God."- Rom. 8:14

The Standard Way
The most important way through which God speaks and by which other ways must be measured is the Word of God; God will never speak outside of His written word.

1. Scriptures:
"All scripture is given by inspiration of God and is profitable for doctrine, for reproof, for correction, for instruction in righteousness" – 2 Tim. 3:16

A. Logos - General/literal word
"This Book of the Law shall not depart from your mouth, but you shall meditate in it day and night, that you may observe to do according to all that is written in it. For then you will make your way prosperous and then you will have good success."-Josh. 1:8

The logos is the written word in the bible (letter) which gives general rules and guidelines on issues such as how God's people should marry and how they should work in such a way that God is glorified, but the bible will never tell you who you should specifically marry or where you should work.

B. Rhema - Specific/Relevant word
"And Peter answered Him and said, "Lord, if it is You, command me to come to You on the water." So He said, "Come." and when Peter had come

down out of the boat, he walked on the water to go to Jesus."-Matt. 14:28-29

The Rhema word speaks of God's specific active and relative word to an individual. It is when the word of God comes alive for an individual such as when he speaks to an individual specifically on things like who to marry, where to work, what church to be a part of. This mainly happens while the Word of God is being read or preached.

The Natural Ways
God also speaks through regular and what may seem like ordinary means.

2. Circumstances
God can and does speak through our everyday circumstances. There are various circumstances through which He can speak; some of which are outlined below:

"But Jonah arose to flee to Tarshish from the presence of the LORD... But the LORD sent out a great wind on the sea and there was a mighty tempest on the sea, so that the ship was about to be broken up."- Jonah 1:1-4

A. Doors:
Sometimes an open door or opportunity could mean God favours a certain decision, but some other times the enemy could encourage or mislead us by creating false opportunities. Hence this medium must be confirmed by one or two other methods through which God speaks.

8"But I will tarry at Ephesus until Pentecost. 9 for a great door and effectual is opened unto me and there are many adversaries." - 1 Cor.16:8-9

B. Seasons:

God could also require us to read the season in order for us to determine the right cause of action for a particular time. We are meant to do the right thing in the right season.

28""Now <u>learn this parable from the fig tree:</u> When its branch has <u>already become tender</u> and <u>puts forth leaves</u>, you <u>know that summer is near</u>.

29 "So you also, <u>when you see these things</u> happening, <u>know that it is near--at the doors!</u>

30 "Assuredly, I say to you, this generation will by no means pass away till all these things take place." – Matthew 13:28-30

C. Events:

While praying to God concerning an issue such as whom we should marry or where we should live, God could cause someone or some incident to "coincidentally" reveal more helpful information that helps guide us into going forward or retreating on the issue.

"14 "Now <u>let it be that the young woman to whom I say, 'Please let down your pitcher</u> that I may drink,' and she says, 'Drink and I will also give your camels a drink' -<u>let her be the one You have appointed for Your servant Isaac.</u> And by this I will know that You have shown kindness to my master."

15 And it happened, before he had finished speaking, that behold, Rebekah, who was born to Bethuel, son of Milcah, the wife of Nahor, Abraham's brother, came out with her pitcher on her shoulder.

16 Now the young woman was very beautiful to behold, a virgin; no man had known her. And she went down to the well, filled her pitcher and came up.

17 And the servant ran to meet her and said, "Please let me drink a little water from your pitcher."

18 <u>So she said, "Drink, my lord." Then she quickly let her pitcher down</u>

to her hand and gave him a drink.
19 And when she had finished giving him a drink, she said, "I will draw
water for your camels also, until they have finished drinking."" – Gen.
24:14-19

HOW NOT TO BE LED BY GOD
i. Fleecing God
As believers, we are not meant to test or set a fleece for God, even
though Gideon did, this is not God's preferred way.

36 So Gideon said to God, "If You will save Israel by my hand as You have
said-
37 "look, I shall put a fleece of wool on the threshing floor; if there is dew
on the fleece only and it is dry on all the ground, then I shall know that You
will save Israel by my hand, as You have said."
38 And it was so. When he rose early the next morning and squeezed the
fleece together, he wrung the dew out of the fleece, a bowlful of water.
Judges 6:36-38

ii. Tempting God
5"Then the devil took Him up into the holy city, set Him on the pinnacle
of the temple,
6 and said to Him, "If You are the Son of God, throw Yourself down. For
it is written: 'He shall give His angels charge over you 'and,' In their hands
they shall bear you up, lest you dash your foot against a stone.' "Jesus said
to him, "It is written again, 'You shall not tempt the LORD your God."-
Matt. 4:5-6

3. Sanctified Common sense (Wisdom)
God has given us a brain so we can use it. He expects us to use our
reasoning ability sometimes and on some occasions.

"And the king said, "Divide the living child in two and give half to one

and half to the other."-1Kings 3:2

A. Desire:

Sometimes, God leads us by granting us the desire of our heart. This usually happens when our desire aligns with His will.

3"Trust in the LORD and do good; dwell in the land and feed on His faithfulness.
4 Delight yourself also in the LORD and He shall give you the desires of your heart." – Psalm 37:3-4

B. Wisdom:

When we pray and ask God for wisdom, we must receive it by faith and expect He will speak through our reasoning abilities

5"If any of you lacks wisdom, let him ask of God, who gives to all liberally and without reproach and it will be given to him.
6 but let him ask in faith, with no doubting, for he who doubts is like a wave of the sea driven and tossed by the wind." - James1:5-6

C. Tests:

We are not meant to test God but we are required to test people's faithfulness before placing them in a position, office or before we are joined to them in marriage.

"But let these also first be tested; then let them serve as deacons, being found blameless." 1 Tim 3:10

HOW NOT TO BE LED BY CIRCUMSTANCES
i. Casting Lots

God is not a gambler and therefore lot casting is not His method of giving direction.

"And they said to one another, "Come, <u>let us cast lots,</u> that we may know for whose cause this trouble has come upon us." So they cast lots and the lot fell on Jonah."- Jonah 1:7

ii. Democracy

While democracy works amongst men, it is not God's way of making a choice for you. It may work within a political system but God is not a politician.

"And they proposed two: Joseph called Barsabas, who was surnamed Justus and Matthias.
And they prayed and said, "You, O Lord, who know the hearts of all, show which of these two You have chosen …And they cast their lots and the lot fell on Matthias. And he was numbered with the eleven apostles. Acts 1:23-26

4. Mentors

God will also speak and direct us through the mouth of mentors and godly counsellors. He can sometimes use both experts in their fields and spiritually mature people to help, advice, guide, or confirm to us His will. This could be particularly helpful and may prove to be invaluable in the choice of a marriage partner.

"Where there is no <u>counsel,</u> the people fall; but in the multitude of <u>counsellors </u>there is safety."
Prov. 11:14

1"Blessed is the man Who walks not in <u>the counsel</u> of the ungodly, Nor stands in the path of sinners, Nor sits in the seat of the scornful;
2 But his delight is in the law of the LORD and in His law he meditates day and night"-Psalm1:1-2

The passage above teaches that we must also be weary of taking ungodly counsel

The Supernatural Ways
5. Impressions
God will many times guide us through an impression in our spirit-man which is sometimes called our intuition. One may have an impression that something might be the case; "he had an intuition that something had gone wrong"

According to Dictionary.com, Intuition is:
- A direct perception of truth, fact, etc., independent of any reasoning process; an immediate apprehension.
- A fact, truth, etc., perceived in this way.
- A keen and quick insight.
- The quality or ability of having such direct perception or quick insight.
- An immediate cognition of an object not inferred or determined by a previous cognition of the same object. Any object or truth so discerned.
- Pure, untaught, no inferential knowledge.
- The capacity for Intuition is a function of the Spirit man and not of the mind.

9"*Now when much time had been spent and sailing was now dangerous because the Fast was already over, Paul advised them,*
10 saying, "Men, I perceive *that* this voyage will end with disaster and much loss, *not only of the cargo and ship, but also our lives."*
11 Nevertheless the centurion was more persuaded by the helmsman and the owner of the ship than by the things spoken by Paul."-Acts27:9-11

What is the Voice of Reason vs. Intuition?
- It is an instinctive knowing (without the use of rational processes)
- It is an immediate apprehension or cognition without reasoning

or inference.

TYPES OF IMPRESSIONS
Checks
A check is a sense of hesitation in our spirit even when our rational mind may say otherwise.

Promptings
A prompt is a stirring in one's spirit-man to move ahead on a certain action or decision even when one's logical or reasoning faculty is saying different.

6. Preaching
"And they said to one another, "Did not <u>our heart burn</u> within us <u>while He talked with us on the road and while He opened the Scriptures</u> to us?"-Luke 24:32

God can and will also speak through His servants (Shepherds) while they teach and preach His word to us.

i. General words
This could come as a general word spoken at the beginning of the year for the congregation by the leader for that particular year.

'Then Elijah said to Ahab, "Go up, eat and drink; for there is <u>the sound of abundance of rain.</u>"' - 1Kings 18:41

ii. Specific words
It is important to know as we are guided by this means that,

• God chooses your Shepherds

"And <u>I will give you shepherds according to My heart</u>, who will feed you

with knowledge and understanding."Then it shall come to pass, when you are multiplied and increased in the land in those days," – Jer. 3:15-16

● We are required to submit to the Shepherds God put over us

"Obey those who rule over you and be submissive, for they watch out for your souls, as those who must give account. Let them do so with joy and not with grief, for that would be unprofitable for you." Heb.13:17

7. Prophecy
"When he had come to us, he took Paul's belt, bound his own hands and feet and said, "Thus says the Holy Spirit, 'So shall the Jews at Jerusalem bind the man who owns this belt and deliver him into the hands of the Gentiles."- Acts 21:10

Prophecy is about declaring what God has revealed. There are three general ways they can be received
i. Descriptive (Word of Knowledge)   e.g. Elisha in 2 Kings6:9-12
ii. Prescriptive (Word of Wisdom) e.g. Joseph in Gen. 41:27-36
iii. Predictive (Prophecy) e.g. Daniel and Agabus in Acts21:11-14

The Spectacular Ways
God also speaks in other spectacular ways which will only be outlined below given they have already being discussed in more details in previous chapters.

8. Dreams
"And a vision (dream) appeared to Paul in the night. A man of Macedonia stood and pleaded with him, saying, "Come over to Macedonia and help us." – Acts 16:9

9. Visions
"About the ninth hour of the day he saw clearly in a vision an angel of God

coming in and saying to him, "Cornelius!"…

5 "Now send men to Joppa and send for Simon whose surname is Peter…10 Then he became very hungry and wanted to eat; but while they made ready, he fell into a trance"- Acts 10: 3-10

10. Audible Voice

"While Peter thought about the vision, <u>the Spirit said to him,</u> "Behold, three men are seeking you.

"Arise therefore, go down and go with them, doubting nothing; for I have sent them."- Acts 10:19-20

How to Fine tune your Spirit

In order to hear God clearly, we need to ensure our spirit-man is sharp, keen and sensitive by ensuring we continually keep it refined and in tune by regularly embarking and maintaining the spiritual disciplines listed below.

1. Fasting
2. Prayer
3. Bible Study
4. Solitude
5. Journaling
6. Worship
7. Obedience

SECTION 3

OPERATING IN
THE PROPHETIC

CHAPTER 10

THE PROPHETIC TOOL KIT

Every tradesman is skilled due to specialist training and is also equipped with the tools of the trade with which he does his work. Carpenters have hammers, nails and saws; plumbers use wrenches and suckers, electricians use screwdrivers and painters use paint brushes. In the same vein, prophets are skilled and have certain tools (gifts and abilities) at their disposal, which God gives them so that they can function in their offices. We are not all called to be prophets but we can all prophesy. In this chapter, we will look at how we can access and function with these prophetic gifts and abilities.

The Keys of the Kingdom

15 "He said to them, "But who do you say that I am?"
16 Simon Peter answered and said, "You are the Christ, the Son of the living God."
17 Jesus answered and said to him, "Blessed are you, Simon Bar-Jonah, <u>for flesh and blood has not revealed this to you,</u> but <u>My Father who is in heaven.</u>

18 "And I also say to you that you are Peter and on this rock I will build My church and <u>the gates of Hades shall not prevail against it.</u>
19 "And <u>I will give you</u> the <u>keys of the kingdom of heaven</u> and whatever you bind on earth will be bound in heaven and whatever you loose on earth will be loosed in heaven."" – Matt. 16:15-18

The scripture above shows us that God gives us keys (tools) to enable us access realms that are otherwise inaccessible to us by natural means. God the Father wants to give us the keys of revelation and authority, like He did to Peter, so that we can bind, cancel and frustrate the enemies' plans and loose, release and facilitate God's plans and purposes on earth. This is so that the church of God may be built and established and the gates of hell (forces of the devil) be disabled from prevailing against it. These keys will open doors previously shut by the enemy and shut doors previously opened by the same.

6"And when Herod was about to bring him out, that night Peter was sleeping, bound with two chains between two soldiers; and the guards before the door were keeping the prison.
7 Now behold, <u>an angel of the Lord</u> stood by him and <u>a light shone in the prison;</u> and he struck Peter on the side and raised him up, saying, "Arise quickly!" <u>And his chains fell off his hands.</u>
8 Then the angel said to him, "Gird yourself and tie on your sandals"; and so he did. And he said to him, "Put on your garment and follow me."
9 So he went out and followed him and did not know that what was done by the angel was real, but thought he was seeing a vision.
10 When they were past the first and the second guard posts, <u>they came to the iron gate that leads to the city,</u> which <u>opened to them of its own accord;</u> and they went out and went down one street and immediately the angel departed from him.
11 And when Peter had come to himself, he said, "Now I know for

certain that <u>the Lord has sent His angel</u> and has <u>delivered me from the</u>
<u>hand of Herod</u> and from all the expectation of the Jewish people." "
Acts12:6-11

The gates of hell could not prevail against Peter and the church
because they had access to many keys. These gifts will be
explored below

Different Tools (Gifts) of the Spirit

"4 There are <u>diversities of gifts</u>, but the same Spirit.
5 There are <u>differences of ministries</u>, but the same Lord.
6 And there are <u>diversities of activities</u>, but it is the same God who
works all in all.
7 But the manifestation of the Spirit is given to each one for the profit
of all:
8 for to one is given the <u>word of wisdom</u> through the Spirit, to another
the <u>word of knowledge</u> through the same Spirit,
9 to another <u>faith</u> by the same Spirit, to another <u>gifts of healings</u> by the
same Spirit,
10 to another the <u>working of miracles,</u> to another <u>prophecy,</u> to another
<u>discerning of spirits</u>, to another <u>different kinds of tongues</u>, to another <u>the</u>
<u>interpretation of tongues</u>.
11 But one and <u>the same Spirit works all these things</u>, distributing to
each one individually <u>as He wills.</u>" – 1Corinth 12:4-11

This scripture shows that there is a retinue of spiritual tools or
keys available to the believer which can be drawn upon or be
released to them by the Holy Spirit as He deems fit depending on
the situation they are dealing with or in which they find
themselves. We don't determine what tools we use in any given
situation. He decides what is required and what to pull out of
the bag, so to say. Each tool (gift) serves a specific function and
fulfils a particular purpose. The 9 spiritual gifts mentioned here

are not exhaustive and can be categorised under 3 major headings:

Revelation gifts
These three are the set of gifts the prophet is usually endowed with and commonly walks in.

Word of Knowledge
Word of Wisdom
Discerning of Spirits

Communication (Utterance) gifts
These gifts are more easily accessible to most believers and are mostly used in communicating with God and receiving instructions from Him in prayer and or communicating with other believers by the Spirit of God.

Prophecy
Tongues
Interpretation of Tongues

Power gifts
This set of gifts is what I call the assault gifts. While the revelatory gifts help us to locate the enemy and his plans and uncover his plots and disguises; the power gifts help us destroy the structures and devises the enemy has set up like diseases, debt, death and depression. These gifts also help rebuild what the enemy has already destroyed.

Faith
Working of Miracles
Gifts of Healing

Testimonies of the Tools and Gifts in action
Many people already operate or have the potential to operate in these gifts and use these tools but unfortunately they either don't know they have them or have not been trained to use them. Many people are given words of knowledge, wisdom, discerning of spirits and even a prophecy in their dreams but either they do not understand the language spoken by the Spirit or they are not aware of how to operate them. Below, I will illustrate the revelation gifts from various practical experiences that I have had.

Word of Knowledge
A word of knowledge is a supernatural revelation of a fact concerning a person or an event to an individual by the Spirit of God that would not have been known otherwise or accessed by the natural mind. A word of knowledge is usually given by God to either unearth the enemy's plans or to astound the individual in question in order to get his or her attention so that God can speak to him or her.

*24 "But if all _prophesy_ and an _unbeliever_ or an _uninformed person_ comes in, he is _convinced_ by all, he is _convicted_ by all.
25 And thus _the secrets of his heart_ are _revealed_; and so, falling down on his face, _he will worship God_ and _report_ that _God is truly among you_." – 1 Corinth.14:24-25*

Boiling kettle and spirit of Anger
After a church service, a crowd of people came to the altar to be prayed for; as I shut my eyes I saw with my mind's eye (pictorial vision) a boiling kettle with steam hissing out from its spout. When I asked if anyone had had an incident with a kettle recently a certain lady said her electric kettle had exploded just the day before and that she was almost badly hurt. I went on to tell her

that I saw a spirit of uncontrollable anger over her. She immediately confirmed that she did have a bad anger problem which sometimes ended in rage and that on one occasion in another church; she had raised a chair and almost threw it at a child in an uncontrolled state of anger while she was teaching in the children's church.

Marital Affair revealed and terminated

The Lord had asked me to warn a lady in my church not to get in touch with a certain old male friend when she travelled. I had forgotten to give her the warning. Three weeks later, while I was scrolling through my phone, I stumbled across her number and was immediately prompted by the Spirit to call her. When she picked up the call, she confirmed that she had indeed made contact with him. I then proceeded to ask if they had been intimate, but she wasn't forthcoming with such information. At that moment, the Spirit of God immediately revealed a dream I had the day before which confirmed they had been intimate. She later confirmed that there had been a level of inappropriate physical contact but that it had not led to full intercourse. That word of knowledge allowed me to counsel and support her marriage so that it was strengthened and not torn apart by adultery.

The Enemy and his plans Uncovered

8 *"Now the king of Syria was <u>making war against Israel</u>; and he consulted with his servants, saying, <u>"My camp will be in such and such a place."</u>*

9 *And <u>the man of God </u>sent to the king of Israel, saying, <u>"Beware that you do not pass this place, for the Syrians are coming down there."</u>*

10 *Then the king of Israel sent someone to the place of which the man of God had told him. Thus he <u>warned him</u> and he <u>was watchful there,</u> not just once or twice.*

11 Therefore the heart of the king of Syria was greatly troubled by this thing; and he called his servants and said to them, "Will you not show me which of us is for the king of Israel?"
12 And one of his servants said, "None, my lord, O king; but Elisha, the prophet who is in Israel, tells the king of Israel the words that you speak in your bedroom." " – 2 Kings 6:8-12

Satan likes to operate under the cloak and cover of darkness. He never likes it when Jesus shines the light on his plans and unveils his activities and thwarts his plans.

Through the instrumentality of the gift of the word of knowledge, Satan and his demons are easily exposed and dealt with, because whenever Light comes in darkness must exit.

Exposing and Breaking Ancestral ties

As we were rounding up a prayer meeting some years ago, I saw in my mind's eye (pictorial vision) a traditional Nigerian King's staff of office fall to the ground. I asked if anyone in the group came from a royal family. A lady who was a new and zealous believer and who loved the Lord raised her hand and further explained that her father was going through his initiation and installation rites in that season as we spoke. I then prayed for her and figuratively began to break off every ancestral tie to any idolatrous throne by the prophetic act of waving my hand in a cutting motion about one foot in front of her navel which represents an umbilical connection with her ancestry. Suddenly, we heard a voice coming from her that wasn't hers - a viscous and wicked spirit spoke vile words from her mouth threatening to destroy her and shook and threw her violently on the ground. It was too late though, the enemy had already been uncovered and exposed. She was delivered by the power of the Lord Jesus

Christ the same day and has grown to become a mighty tool in God's hand.

Various attempts to terminate people's lives and destinies by the spirit of death, accidents or disease have been uncovered and terminated by the gift of the word of knowledge in action.

Word of Wisdom
The word of wisdom is a supernatural revelation by the Spirit of God to the mind of a person instructing them on what to do or how to solve a problem or what direction to take in a particular situation. It is like a wise word from the Spirit of God.

Launch out into the Deep!
About 5 years ago, I was invited to a very little church of not more than 15 people as a guest speaker at their conference. While I was enjoying the very vibrant and sincere worship, I heard a clear word in the ear of my spirit by the Spirit of God which was, "Launch out into the deep for a big catch of fish". He later explained that my ministry had only operated in shallow waters until then and that I needed to launch out by faith into deeper realms in the supernatural to see the wonders of the deep. He then said, "You don't catch big fish in shallow waters, launch out!" This word of wisdom is what gave birth to a regular miracle service we themed the 'Solution Night' which saw many people healed, delivered from bondages and receive phenomenal testimonies.

£150,000 flat sold to build God's house
About 8 years ago, when we had just taken over a building to be used as our new church premises, I took about 80 church workers to pray in the building. While we were worshiping, the Spirit of God revealed to me by a word of knowledge that someone was

about to sell a property for £150,000 and the Lord revealed to me clearly that the profits from the sale was to be used to renovate the new building. Unknown to me, one of those present was selling a flat for that amount and God had already told them that the proceeds were to go to the new church building, so the word of wisdom was a confirmation for them.

Discerning of Spirits

The gift of discerning of spirits is a supernatural revelation by the Holy Spirit that makes us aware of the spiritual atmosphere and gives us insight into the particular kind of Spirit operating in the atmosphere. This gift helps ascertain whether angels, demons, Satan or even God's Spirit Himself are present in a place or person. It can also discern the dominating influence of a human spirit in a place or person.

Divine (Godly) Spirits

The Presence of God

With the gift of discerning of spirits, people can sense when the presence of God enters a room or the anointing of God is upon a person. Being aware of God's presence will enable the individual to respond appropriately.

16"Then Jacob awoke from his sleep and said, "Surely the LORD is in this place and I did not know it."
17 And he was afraid and said, "How awesome is this place! This is none other than the house of God and this is the gate of heaven!"
18 Then Jacob rose early in the morning and took the stone that he had put at his head, set it up as a pillar and poured oil on top of it.
19 And he called the name of that place Bethel; but the name of that city had been Luz previously.

20 Then <u>Jacob made a vow, saying, "If God will be with me and keep</u> <u>me in this way that I am going and</u> give me bread to eat and clothing to put on," – Gen 28:16-20

In a church service sometimes I am able to ascertain when the presence of God is present to heal people or when there is an open heaven.

17"Now it happened on a certain day, as He was teaching, that there were Pharisees and teachers of the law sitting by, who had come out of every town of Galilee, Judea and Jerusalem. <u>And the power of the Lord</u> <u>was present to heal them.</u>
18 Then behold, men brought on a bed a man who was paralyzed, whom they sought to bring in and lay before Him.
19 And when they could not find how they might bring him in, because of the crowd, they went up on the housetop and let him down with his bed through the tiling into the midst before Jesus." – Luke 5:17-19

Angelic presence
This gift also helps one know or even see when angels are present in a place and ready to act on one's behalf.

"And Elisha prayed and said, "LORD, I pray, <u>open his eyes that he</u> <u>may see</u>." Then the LORD opened the eyes of the young man and he saw. And behold, the mountain <u>was full of horses and chariots of fire all</u> <u>around Elisha</u>."- 2 Kings 6:17

Demonic (Evil) spirits
The gift of discerning of spirits can also help discern the presence of evil spirits in a place or upon a person.

16"Now it happened, as we went to prayer, that a certain slave girl <u>possessed with a spirit of divination</u> met us, who <u>brought her masters</u>

much profit by fortune-telling.
17 This girl followed Paul and us and cried out, saying, "These men are the servants of the Most High God, who proclaim to us the way of salvation."
18 And this she did for many days. But <u>Paul, greatly annoyed, turned and <u>said to the spirit, "I command you in the name of Jesus Christ to come out of her."</u> And <u>he came out that very hour."</u> – Acts 16:16-18

Witchcraft activity in the house

Many years ago, the gift of discerning of spirit came upon me strongly while I was spending the night at a friend's house. While my friend and a relative of his were watching TV late into the night, I suddenly started feeling very drowsy, like I had been drugged even though I was not physically tired or sleepy. I struggled with this strange drowsy feeling for some minutes as I knew the lulling effect was coming from outside of me. Even though my eyes were shut, I suddenly saw an image of an old lady come out like a thick fog out of my friend's relative. This was shocking as in reality she was a young lady. This spirit literally came out of her side and pinched me on my hip joint. The pain I felt was as if someone had taken a sharp nail and used a hammer to drive into my hip joint. I got up from the chair and limped into the bedroom (I limped for a few days after the incident). When I got into the bedroom I started to pray intensely and my friend and this relative of his couldn't enter the room despite much effort even though the door was open. They said there was fire in the room.

Demonic presence in the room

While still in this friend's house, I paced up and down and prayed in the room I was in. When I walked past certain parts of the room I would feel a drain of spiritual virtue. When I looked behind the curtain around where I felt virtue leave me, I would find a fetish charm or talisman hidden there. A fetish object is one that is used in voodoo or black magic practices to cast spells. It is an inanimate object that has become an embodiment and habitation of evil spirits or magical powers. It is usually planted in places for demonic protection or to wreck havoc on people who come by the area.

When I identified these objects I threw them out and the evil presence would reduce in intensity. I discovered and disposed of about 4 of these in the room. I also noticed some very strong lustful spirits or witchcraft spirits coming from some but not all of the photographs that were on the wall in this room. When I took down these particular photos, the intensity of the demonic presence diminished and only then was I able to finally sleep in peace that night.

Prevailing spirit in a place
Certain places are known for particular vices; for example Las Vegas is known for gambling, San Francisco is known for homosexuality and Amsterdam for drugs and prostitution.

People who operate in the gift of discerning of spirits are able to pick up the dominant spirit controlling a particular place.

The gift of discerning of spirits is a very instrumental key in helping us to be more targeted and strategic in our prayers during spiritual warfare or to help discern the dominant spirit in a place when we want to change the spiritual climate in a certain place.

Stirring up your Prophetic gift
As these various divine encounters illustrate, it is possible to walk in a revelatory realm in which God makes these tools available to you. How do you begin to utilise these tools?

The responsibility of the development of the prophetic gift is with the young prophet. As Paul admonished Timothy not to neglect his gift, but to stir it up, so are we required to stir up our prophetic gift though prayer, fasting, worship and the exercise and use of these gifts by faith.

"6 Therefore I remind you to <u>stir up the gift of God</u> which is in you through the laying on of my hands."- 2 Tim.1:6

Developing your Prophetic gift

"12 For though by this time you <u>ought to be teachers,</u> you <u>need someone to teach you again</u> the first principles of the oracles of God; and you have come <u>to need milk</u> and <u>not solid food</u>.

13 For everyone who partakes only of <u>milk</u> is <u>unskilled in the word</u> of righteousness, for he is a <u>babe</u>.

14 But <u>solid food</u> belongs to those who are of <u>full age</u>, that is, those who by <u>reason of use</u> have their <u>senses exercised</u> to <u>discern</u> both good and evil."- Heb. 5:12-14

You develop your prophetic gift like a baby learns to walk. The baby is prepared for walking by being fed a nutritious diet (likewise you start the prophetic journey by eating the commensurate diet for your level). Everyone who desires the prophetic must start by reading the scriptures; this is like a baby learning to crawl. As you read the scripture, you learn about God and begin to be familiar with how He talks. The next stage is to go from reading the scripture to studying the scripture. You study the scriptures by not just reading the scriptures but also asking questions as you read. It is important to ask why certain things happen and to note behaviours or personalities that invoke certain things. For example, in Acts 16:24-26, we note that when Paul and Silas prayed and praised in prison, the foundations of the prison were shaken. As you study, ask questions such as – what are foundations, what is the significance of the scripture saying that foundations and not just the walls of the prison were shaken and suchlike? This can be likened to a child learning to walk by holding on to chairs. As you study and meditate in scripture and commune with God, He will begin to speak to you about yourself and some times, other people. At this stage, you must be willing to take some risks by stepping out and sharing what you hear with those concerned. This can be likened to a child stepping out to walk without holding on to anything. You don't learn to walk by sitting down – you need to stand up and take a step. You need to begin to share a few impressions or dreams that you have – stepping out in faith by communicating the visions you receive from God. Like learning to walk, the prophetic gifting is perfected by practice. You take a few steps, fall down, get up and try again (i.e. you share the impression or dream, give one or two words that don't come to pass or are inaccurate but you share many more that are accurate and you become encouraged in using the prophetic gift). It is important to reach out in faith and use your gift or it may atrophy.

CHAPTER 11

THE MAKING
OF A PROPHET

Can everyone and anyone become a prophet? No. Even those born to be prophets have to be raised into it or trained into the office. What I share here is my personal journey and experience and every individual's experience will be different. I know that there are lessons that can be gleaned by others from my experience. I never desired to be a prophet; I just discovered I was one. In fact, if it was all left to me, I would have preferred the less controversial and more refined calling of a teacher, but we don't have a choice in the matter - God has the last say.

My Journey
I became a Christian in a room by myself on the eve of my 21st birthday at midnight on the 21st of March 1990. I was filled with the Holy Spirit 21 days later and began to hear God speak expressly from then on. I spoke in tongues and started to pray

fervently. I experienced the privilege of being led moment by moment and warned and guided by the Holy Spirit. On a daily basis as I prayed, studied scripture and fasted, I experienced the power and presence of God in open and closed visions, the gifts of word of knowledge, discerning of spirits and the gift of interpretation. All this happened even before I knew what they meant.

1"Then the boy Samuel ministered to the LORD before Eli. And the word of the LORD was rare in those days; there was no widespread revelation.

2 And it came to pass at that time, while Eli was lying down in his place and when his eyes had begun to grow so dim that he could not see,

3 and before the lamp of God went out in the tabernacle of the LORD where the ark of God was and while Samuel was lying down,

4 that the LORD called Samuel. And he answered, "Here I am!"…. 1 Sam. 3: 1-4

The Supernatural encounters

Early in my walk with God, within the first couple of weeks I had encounters with witchcraft and soon discovered that the powers of darkness were no match for the Holy Spirit.

On the 1st of May 1990, I had a trance-like experience in which I saw God reveal to me how a dark cloak or curse had been brought upon the nation of my birth by some of the nation's past leaders. On August 17th of the same year, I had an open vision where I saw an ostrich with its head buried in the ground, a vision which I only began to understand after the terrorist attacks of September 11 2001 (11 years later). At this time, I definitely did not see myself as a prophet or think my experiences were prophetic; I just really loved God and wanted to do His will.

The 'Bread Bible' experience

In my zeal to do the will of God and serve Him, I became the founding pastor of a Christian fellowship on the 5th of March 1991 while also serving as an intern doctor in a teaching hospital. After concluding my housemanship and pastorate of this new fellowship, I began to pray and ask God for direction for the next phase of ministry. In an open vision, He showed me a picture of a cake or sweet bread baked in the shape of a bible. The bible looked so delicious I really wanted to eat it all up. When I shared this experience with a couple of older Christian friends some days later, I was informed that there was a similar story in scripture in Ezek3:1-4.

"1 Moreover He said to me, "Son of man, eat what you find; <u>eat this scroll and <u>go, speak to the house of Israel</u>."</u> 2 So I opened my mouth and He caused me to eat that scroll.
3 And He said to me, "<u>Son of man, feed your belly and fill your stomach with this scroll that I give you.</u>" So I ate and it was in my mouth like honey in sweetness.
4 Then He said to me: "Son of man, <u>go to the house of Israel and speak with My words to them.</u> 5 For you are not sent to a people of unfamiliar speech and of hard language, but to the house of Israel," – Ezekiel 3:1-4*

On reading this passage, it became clear for the first time that God was raising me up to be a prophet (His spoke person). He was requesting that I read, study, digest, assimilate and embody the scriptures in preparation for the role as His spokesman. A few months later, I discovered there was another passage in the New Testament, Revelations 10:5-13 which was very similar to the one in Ezekiel 3:1-4.

"8 Then the voice which I heard from heaven spoke to me again and said, "Go, take the little book which is open in the hand of the angel who stands on the sea and on the earth."
9 So I went to the angel and said to him, "Give me the little book."
And he said to me, "Take and eat it; and it will make your stomach bitter, but it will be as sweet as honey in your mouth."
10 Then I took the little book out of the angel's hand and ate it and it was as sweet as honey in my mouth. But when I had eaten it, my stomach became bitter. 11 And he[b] said to me, "You must prophesy again about many peoples, nations, tongues and kings.""
Revelations 10:8-10

This passage further confirmed God's call to me, as the scripture says everything should be confirmed by the mouth of two or three witnesses. Both Ezekiel and John the Revelatory were key "Seer Prophets" who were pivotal in bringing far reaching prophetic words to God's people.

Experiencing Supernatural Power and Authority
A few months after the experience detailed above, I moved from Ibadan to Lagos which is the main commercial city and hub of Nigeria. I began working as a junior doctor in a private hospital. At this time, I also began to read and study about a believer's spiritual authority and power. I had experienced the God that reveals and exposes evil spirits and their human agents but I was yet to experience the power of the God who can deliver the oppressed from demonic bondages. I began to listen to Derek Prince and Bill Subritzky's audio and video messages on deliverance from demonic oppression and the breaking of curses.

"17 And these signs will follow those who believe: In My name they will cast out demons; they will speak with new tongues; 18 they[a] will take up serpents; and if they drink anything deadly, it will by no means

hurt them; they will lay hands on the sick and they will recover." –
Mark 16:17-18

As a result, within a couple of weeks I began to experience an increased spiritual authority for people I prayed for. I began to see that some people would manifest demons even when I just preached or prayed simple prayers. I began to see patients in the hospital I worked in get delivered from demonic oppression, healed and saved.

Developing my Prophetic gift
After a brief stint working as a medical doctor, I left medicine and started a design and print promotions business, while I continued as a lay minister with my home church. In that period, I helped to start a new church plant and founded another Christian fellowship on a medical campus which I pastored for about a year. While leading this fellowship, I was introduced to a book by my Pastor titled, "Developing your Prophetic gift" by Graham Cooke. This book served as the first text on developing ones prophetic gift that I read. The book went a long way in helping me further discover, develop, apply and confirm my revelatory gifting. This is where I discovered that there are three levels of the gifting and it took a number of years to grow from one level into another.

The Gift of prophecy takes between 0-5 years to develop
The Ministry of the Prophet takes from 5-15 years
The Office of the Prophet matures in about 15-20 years.
Mark Poole states that it takes approximately 20 years for God to mature and develop a full Prophet.

Understanding the language of Dreams
In 1995, I was sent by my pastor from Lagos to assist in a church

in London called Jesus House. A year later, I was asked to start a church which I planted with 6 people on January 13th 1996. This church grew by the grace and favour of God. It was in my 7th year of pastoring Trinity Chapel (2003) that I first discovered the ability to interpret dreams. I stumbled upon a tape set produced by a popular "Seer Prophet" called John Paul Jackson. Learning the skill of dream interpretation greatly increased my ability to help people know and understand the will of God.

Mantle, Ministry & Message shift

In 2004, Trinity Chapel moved from a cinema we rented for our services into a building we used exclusively for church which we named the "Leadership Centre". At this time, we also started our TV ministry. My personal assistant, at the time, had a significant dream. In the dream, he saw me preaching wearing 3 layers of clothing. The first layer was lilac in colour and it was worn back to front. Underneath that layer, he noticed that I was wearing a light blue shirt with a tie facing the right way forward. As I broke down the elements of the dream I noted that clothes generally depict ones mantle or authority. I then discovered that lilac (light purple) is the colour that represents leadership and blue represents the prophetic or supernatural. The backward direction of the clothes I interpreted as speaking of the past (i.e. facing the back/that which is behind) and forward facing clothes as speaking of the future (that which is to come).

Leadership to Prophetic

I felt the dream was showing that God was causing a major shift in my mantle, ministry and message. My emphasis until then was primarily on leadership, development and influence; but this dream and my increasingly prophetic experiences indicated that God was moving me into a greater emphasis on the prophetic. God was also moving me from the realm of being an 'echo' (one who repeats what others have said) to becoming a 'voice' (one with an original message).

27"And in these days <u>prophets came</u> from Jerusalem to <u>Antioch.</u>
28 Then one of them, named Agabus, <u>stood up</u> and <u>showed by the Spirit</u> that there <u>was going to be a great famine throughout all the world,</u> which <u>also happened</u> in the days of Claudius Caesar.
29 Then the disciples, each according to his ability, determined to send relief to the brethren dwelling in Judea.
30 This they also did and sent it to the elders by the hands of Barnabas and Saul."
Acts 11:27-30

We see in the passage above that as the church in Antioch matured, the emphasis of the ministry in Antioch shifted from purely teaching to incorporate the prophetic. Likewise, I sensed at Trinity Chapel, that God was moving us from a teaching focused church to one which also embraced the prophetic. It was comforting to come across this scripture and realise that God can start a ministry off with a certain focus or message and eventually shift them into, or include, another.

My Transition from "Teacher" to "Prophet"

The Office of Teacher
The Fruit of a Teacher is trained disciples and transformed character

25"Then Barnabas departed for Tarsus to seek Saul.
26 And when he had found him, he brought him to Antioch. So it was that for a whole year they assembled with the church <u>and taught a great many people</u>. And <u>the disciples</u> were first called <u>Christians in</u> Antioch."- Acts 11:25-26

In the passage above, we can conclude that though Apostle Paul was called as an Apostle, he first started out in his ministry as a Teacher and the effectiveness of his teaching ministry was evidenced by the disciples that had become Christ-like. In fact, they were so Christ-like that they were the first set of believers to be called Christians.

The Office of the Prophet

The Fruit of a Prophet is revelation, warning and manifestation of what was revealed.

In Acts 11:27, (quoted a few paragraphs above) we see that Agabus had prophetically picked up a famine before it happened. The same scripture also confirms that it happened just as he had predicted

The True Test of a Prophet

The revelation of the fact before it happens and the confirmation by the occurrence of the event is the hallmark of a true prophet. Deuteronomy 18:21-22 confirms that the test of a real prophet is not in his/her title or his/her words but rather in the performance and fulfilment of his/her words.

"21 And if you say in your heart, 'How shall we know the word which the LORD has not spoken?' — 22 when a prophet speaks in the name of the LORD, if the thing does not happen or come to pass, that is the thing which the LORD has not spoken; the prophet has spoken it presumptuously; you shall not be afraid of him." - Deuteronomy 18:21-22

As a prophet grows, develops and matures he will soon develop a reputation for the performance of his words.

"....19 So Samuel grew and the LORD was with him and let none of his words fall to the ground.

20 And all Israel from Dan to Beersheba knew that Samuel had been established as a prophet of the LORD.

21 Then the LORD appeared again in Shiloh. For the LORD revealed Himself to Samuel in Shiloh by the word of the LORD. 1 Sam.. 3:19-21

4:1 And the word of Samuel came to all Israel."- 1 Sam. 4:1

Prophetic Visitation... Storms are coming!!!

One of the most defining encounters of my prophetic journey is a visitation I had in January 2005 where God showed me a season and series of storms that were coming which would devastate and shake many to their foundations. I responded by preaching it as a warning message to my church which was broadcast and recorded. When the same message was played 5 years later every word spoken had literally come to pass.

CHAPTER 12

UNDERSTANDING THE ROLE OF A PROPHETIC WATCHMAN

1"Again the word of the LORD came to me, saying,
2 "Son of man, speak to the children of your people and say to them:
'When I bring the sword upon a land and the people of the land <u>take a</u>
<u>man from their territory</u> and <u>make him their watchman,</u>
3 '<u>when he sees the sword coming</u> upon the land, if he blows the
trumpet and <u>warns the people,</u>"-Ezek. 33:1-3

This scripture makes it clear that being a prophetic watchman is a critical role. S/he has the job of standing guard to pick up signals and messages from the "heavenlies" and communicate it to the people in order to save them from impending disaster or destruction.

The History of Watching

The old English word wæccan means to "keep watch, be awake, or remain awake". From as far back as 1539 'a group officially patrolling a town (esp. at night) to keep order, etc." is recorded and a watchdog is recorded from 1610.

What does it mean to 'Watch'?

To watch implies being aware of things around one by perceiving them through the eyes. To watch is to be a spectator, to look on or observe, or to fix attention upon during passage of time. Let's look at the definition in some more detail below.

1. It means to <u>be alertly on the lookout</u>, look attentively, or observe, so as <u>to see what comes</u>, is done, or happens.

1"I will <u>stand my watch</u> and set myself on the rampart and <u>watch to see</u> what He will say to me and what I will answer when I am corrected.
2 Then the LORD answered me and said: "<u>Write the vision</u> and make it plain on tablets, that he may run who reads it.
3 For the vision is <u>yet for an appointed time</u>;"- Habakkuk 2:1-3

2. It also means to look or <u>wait attentively and expectantly,</u> to <u>watch for a signal</u> or to <u>watch for an opportunity</u>.

30""Assuredly, I say to you, this generation will by no means pass away <u>till all these things take place.</u>
31 "Heaven and earth will pass away, but My words will by no means pass away.
32 "<u>But of that day and hour no one knows</u>, not even the angels in heaven, nor the Son, but only the Father.
33 "<u>Take heed, watch and pray</u>; for <u>you do not know when the time is.</u>
34 "It is like a man going to a far country, who left his house and gave authority to his servants and <u>to each his work</u> and <u>commanded the</u>

doorkeeper to watch.
35 "*Watch therefore, for you do not know when the master of the house is coming--in the evening, at midnight, at the crowing of the rooster, or in the morning--*
36 "*lest, coming suddenly, he find you sleeping.*
37 "*And what I say to you, I say to all: Watch!*" "- *Mark 13:30-37*

Other meanings are given below:

3. To be careful or cautious – e.g. 'Watch when you cross the street'.

4. To keep awake, especially for a purpose; to remain vigilant, in order to protect or keep safe or to watch over a sick person, a minor or a prisoner for example.

"*And when Herod was about to bring him out, that night Peter was sleeping, bound with two chains between two soldiers; and the guards before the door were keeping the prison.*"- *Acts 12:6*

5. To keep vigil i.e. for devotional purposes.

6. To keep guard e.g. 'He was assigned to watch at the door'.

"*He who scatters has come up before your face. Man the fort! Watch the road! Strengthen your flanks! Fortify your power mightily.*"- *Nahum 2:1*

7. To keep under attentive view or observation, as in order to see or learn something, to view attentively or with interest or to watch a play or game.

8. To contemplate or regard mentally, i.e. to observe a person's

progress.

9. To look or wait attentively and expectantly for i.e. to watch for an opportunity.

10. To keep close, continuous observation for the purpose of seeing or discovering something.

34" "But take heed to yourselves, lest your hearts be weighed down with carousing, drunkenness and cares of this life and that Day come on you unexpectedly.
35 "For it will come as a snare on all those who dwell on the face of the whole earth.
36 "Watch therefore and pray always that you may be counted worthy to escape all these things that will come to pass and to stand before the Son of Man." "- Luke 21:33-36

11. Vigilant guard, as for protection or restraint: to keep watch for prowlers.

"And I said to them, "Do not let the gates of Jerusalem be opened until the sun is hot; and while they stand guard, let them shut and bar the doors; and appoint guards from among the inhabitants of Jerusalem, one at his watch station and another in front of his own house." "- Neh. 7:3

12. A keeping awake for some special purpose e.g. a watch beside a sickbed.

13. A specific period of time for watching or keeping guard i.e. to stand the first watch.

Other types of watches

A watch as it relates to a ship and its crew
a. Any four-hour period beginning at midnight and again at noon during which part of a ship's crew are on duty.
b. Those officers and crew on duty during a specified watch
c. The period during which a guard is on duty e.g. a watch was posted at sunset.
d. A person or group that watches, as a lookout, guard, or sentinel.

A watch of a weather team
A storm watch is meteorological announcement from the national weather service alerting the public that dangerous weather conditions are a possibility and that vigilance and precautionary preparations are advised e.g. a hurricane watch or a tornado watch. Many famous hurricanes were detected before they hit and warnings were sent out e.g. the warning before Hurricane Katrina.

1"Again the word of the LORD came to me, saying,
2 "Son of man, speak to the children of your people and say to them: 'When I bring the sword upon a land and the people of the land take a man from their territory and make him their watchman,
3 'when he sees the sword coming upon the land, if he blows the trumpet and warns the people,..."- Ezek. 33:1-3

Watching and Praying
"40 Then He came to the disciples and found them asleep and said to Peter, "What? Could you not watch with Me one hour?
41 "Watch and pray, lest you enter into temptation. The spirit indeed is willing, but the flesh is weak.""- Matthew 26:40- 41

The reason I have spent so much time explaining the definition of watching is to give full understanding due to its importance. One of the main ways a prophetic person watches is by praying and being spiritually alert to detect responses to prayers. In this way, a prophet can be forewarned and thus forearmed.

Who is Watchman?
The word "Watch" conjures up images of alertness, vigilance and a preparedness and readiness to respond to that which has been sensed in the appropriate time and way. A watchman is therefore an individual who has been chosen and appointed to stand alert, prepared and ready in a particular place or sphere for a particular period in time in order to warn, prepare, intervene or respond appropriately accordingly to external stimuli.
God reveals so we can intervene and take responsibility for what He has shown to us in prayer.

We can be watchmen over our own lives, families, communities, cities or nations.

Understanding your scope and sphere of Prophetic influence

What is your Territory?
1"*Again the word of the LORD came to me, saying,*
 2 *"Son of man, speak to the children of your people and say to them: 'When I bring the sword upon a land and the people of the land <u>take a man from their territory</u> and <u>make him their watchman,</u>*
 3 *'<u>when he sees the sword coming</u> upon the land, if he blows the trumpet and <u>warns the people,</u>…"- Ezek. 33:1-3*

Spiritual Jurisdiction

God reveals things to people that are within their parameters of authority. That means God reveals things to people concerning the places they are situated (geographically) or connected to or about people over whom they have spiritual oversight. God also reveals information about people to whom we are related or connected to e.g. friends, associates and work colleagues. God revealed what He planned to do to Sodom and Gomorrah to Abraham because his nephew Lot lived there (Abraham had spiritual and family ties and oversight over him and was therefore responsible for him). As a result, Abraham had the authority to intervene in the impending destruction of Sodom and Gomorrah, because he had a stake within that territory.

Spiritual Covering

I have had God reveal things to me either about members of my congregation when I was on holiday thousands of miles away or about people who were once members of the church I led who had relocated to other countries. This is purely because I was spiritually responsible for their oversight and God needed me to intervene in their situation.

Lady in Danger

Every pastor is called to be a watchman over his congregation. God can reveal information to pastors who are spiritually sensitive and watchful about members of their congregation and their community. A number of years ago, the Lord showed me a lady in our congregation. In the dream, I saw her lying down on a bed next to an open window. Shortly after, when I looked outside the same window, I saw a large swarm of locusts approaching the window at top speed and about to invade the room she was in. I woke up from the dream anxious and in shock. I contacted her and told her about the dream. I asked if there was anything she was involved in that was untoward or sinful. She initially said no but after some careful thought she mentioned that she had recently gotten close to a married man and become emotionally attached to him. I then understood that the dream was a warning dream from God revealing that danger was imminent. The emotional adultery she was involved in was leading her into a whirlwind of reprisals. Locusts speak of judgement or punishment or a curse that comes as a consequence of sinful action. It appears that her sin had opened the door to demonic entities and attracted divine judgement.

"'Or else, *if you refuse* to let My people go, behold, tomorrow *I will bring locusts into your territory*."- Exodus 10:4

"For they would come up with their livestock and their tents, coming in *as numerous as locusts*; both they and their camels were without number; and *they would enter the land* to *destroy it*." – Judges 6:5

""When I shut up heaven and there is no rain, or command the locusts to devour the land, or send pestilence among My people,"- 2 Chronicle 7:13

I believe that God revealed the incident to me as her pastor so that I could warn her of the gravity of what she was doing and intercede for her to invoke God's mercy instead of judgement. This is an example of spiritual oversight and covering.

This is what spiritual covering is really all about. Do you know you could actually leave a church or family out of strife and your spiritual covering before God could still remain with the person with whom you are in contention with?

Lot leaves his Spiritual Covering

The passage below documents how Lot left Abraham for what he thought were greener pastures.

"5 Lot also, who went with Abram, had flocks and herds and tents.
6 Now the land was not able to support them, that they might dwell together, for their possessions were so great that they could not dwell together.
7 And there was strife between the herdsmen of Abram's livestock and the herdsmen of Lot's livestock. The Canaanites and the Perizzites then dwelt in the land.
8 So Abram said to Lot, "Please let there be no strife between you and me and between my herdsmen and your herdsmen; for we are brethren.
9 "Is not the whole land before you? Please separate from me. If you take the left, then I will go to the right; or, if you go to the right, then I will go to the left."
10 And Lot lifted his eyes and saw all the plain of Jordan, that it was well watered everywhere (before the LORD destroyed Sodom and Gomorrah) like the garden of the LORD, like the land of Egypt as you go toward Zoar.
11 Then Lot chose for himself all the plain of Jordan and Lot journeyed east. And they separated from each other.
12 Abram dwelt in the land of Canaan and Lot dwelt in the cities of the plain and pitched his tent even as far as Sodom.
13 But the men of Sodom were exceedingly wicked and sinful against the LORD."
Gen. 13:5-13

Abraham still Covers (Watches over) Lot Spiritually
However, Abraham's relationship with God would lead to his life (Lot's) being spared.

17 "And the LORD said, "Shall I hide from Abraham what I am doing,
18 "since Abraham shall surely become a great and mighty nation and

all the nations of the earth shall be blessed in him?... 20 And the LORD said, "Because the outcry against Sodom and Gomorrah is great and because their sin is very grave,

21 "I will go down now and see whether they have done altogether according to the outcry against it that has come to Me; and if not, I will know."

22 Then the men turned away from there and went toward Sodom, but Abraham still stood before the LORD."-Gen18:18-20

Should I expose all his Sins? Understanding Prophetic Protocol
Over the years, the prophetic ministry has taken quite a beating and received a lot of bad press. Prophets have generally being seen as rude, crude and destructive, lacking in people and social skills. This is because they mostly just receive revelation from God and were hardly ever concerned about getting the wisdom for the delivery of the word of revelation.

When I was a much younger believer, I had a lot of Divine encounters and clear revelations about people and their secret lives and intentions but I had not yet developed the wisdom and skill for the proper delivery of a prophetic word. I was more passionate about telling God's truth without the compassion or an understanding of how to *"speak the truth in love"*

Paul admonishes us in the scriptures to only say that which builds other people up and always seek to build other people up.

Love is the guiding principle
"15 but, speaking the truth in love, may grow up in all things into Him who is the head — Christ — 16 from whom the whole body, joined and knit together by what every joint supplies, according to the effective working by which every part does its share, causes growth of the body

for the edifying of itself in love." – Ephesians 4:15-16

God is love and He wants us to be and do everything from the disposition of love. Many people tend to want to mimic the prophets of the Old Testament who frequently brought words of judgement from the Lord. When Jesus came, His mission was "Redemptive" and not "Punitive". He brought the "Law of Love" and came to *"to seek and save that which is lost"*. Yes God still does correct and confronts but He does it in order to convict and not to condemn.

When Jesus spoke to the Samaritan woman at the well in John 4:1-20, He revealed and confronted her about her serial divorces, (she had divorced 5 times); but He also addressed the deeper issues and cravings of her heart that led her into this destructive behaviour. By the time the woman left Jesus' presence she left better instead of being bitter.

Jesus also knew the woman caught in adultery was guilty but His response to her was to *"Go and sin no more"*. This is really radical especially when the Old Testament response to a woman being caught in adultery is stoning to death Leviticus 20:10

When God reveals things about those in Authority over us

10"Now the LORD came and stood and called as at other times, "Samuel! Samuel!" And Samuel answered, "Speak, for Your servant hears."

11 Then the LORD said to Samuel: "Behold, I will do something in Israel at which both ears of everyone who hears it will tingle.

12 "In that day <u>I will perform against Eli all that I have spoken concerning his house, from beginning to end.</u>

13 "For I have told him <u>that I will judge his house forever for the iniquity which he knows, because his sons made themselves vile and he</u>

did not restrain them.

14 "*And therefore I have sworn to the house of Eli that the iniquity of Eli's house shall not be atoned for by sacrifice or offering forever.*"

15 *So Samuel lay down until morning and opened the doors of the house of the LORD. And Samuel was afraid to tell Eli the vision.*

16 *Then Eli called Samuel and said, "Samuel, my son!" And he answered, "Here I am."*

17 *And he said, "What is the word that the LORD spoke to you? Please do not hide it from me. God do so to you and more also, if you hide anything from me of all the things that He said to you."*

18 *Then Samuel told him everything and hid nothing from him. And he said, "It is the LORD. Let Him do what seems good to Him.""*-1 *Sam. 3:10-18*

God will not usually reveal things about our leaders to us because He would usually desire to honour their office. However, when He does it, it is so that;

a. We can intercede for them (cover them in prayer)
b. We can skilfully bring it to their knowledge
c. They can be warned of impending judgement.

I will now deal with the handling of sensitive information as I talk about Prophetic protocol and etiquette. It is important to note that sometimes, God reveals such things in order to test us – to see whether we are matured and good willed enough to handle the information in a way that covers and honours while striving for improvement in the leader.

Delivering a Prophetic Word to people in Authority

Guiding principles in Scripture

1. Do not rebuke an elder
2. Speak the truth in love
3. The Spirit of Gentleness

Wisdom in the delivery of a Prophetic word

When delivering a prophetic word to a person in authority, one must ensure that we do not only speak the truth in love but we do so with respect and preserving the honour of their office. Nathan skilfully delivered a prophetic word of God's judgement to King David while preserving the king's honour and respecting his office without taking away from God's message.

1*"Then the LORD sent Nathan to David. And he came to him and said to him: "There were two men in one city, one rich and the other poor.*
2 "The rich man had exceedingly many flocks and herds.
3 "But the poor man had nothing, except one little ewe lamb which he had bought and nourished; and it grew up together with him and with his children. It ate of his own food and drank from his own cup and lay in his bosom; and it was like a daughter to him.
4 "And a traveller came to the rich man, who refused to take from his own flock and from his own herd to prepare one for the wayfaring man who had come to him; but he took the poor man's lamb and prepared it for the man who had come to him."
5 So David's anger was greatly aroused against the man and he said to Nathan, "As the LORD lives, the man who has done this shall surely die!
6 "And he shall restore fourfold for the lamb, because he did this thing and because he had no pity."
*7 Then Nathan said to David, **"You are the man!** Thus says the*

LORD God of Israel: 'I anointed you king over Israel and I delivered you from the hand of Saul.

8 'I gave you your master's house and your master's wives into your keeping and gave you the house of Israel and Judah. And if that had been too little, I also would have given you much more!

9 'Why have you despised the commandment of the LORD, to do evil in His sight? You have killed Uriah the Hittite with the sword; you have taken his wife to be your wife and have killed him with the sword of the people of Ammon.

10 'Now therefore, the sword shall never depart from your house, because you have despised Me and have taken the wife of Uriah the Hittite to be your wife.'

11 "Thus says the LORD: 'Behold, I will raise up adversity against you from your own house; and I will take your wives before your eyes and give them to your neighbor and he shall lie with your wives in the sight of this sun.

12 'For you did it secretly, but I will do this thing before all Israel, before the sun.'"

13 So David said to Nathan, "I have sinned against the LORD." And Nathan said to David, "The LORD also has put away your sin; you shall not die.

14 "However, because by this deed you have given great occasion to the enemies of the LORD to blaspheme, the child also who is born to you shall surely die."

15 Then Nathan departed to his house. And the LORD struck the child that Uriah's wife bore to David and it became ill.

16 David therefore pleaded with God for the child and David fasted and went in and lay all night on the ground."- 2 Sam. 12:1-15

Parameters of Prophetic Authority (Levels of Spiritual Authority)

As mentioned above, God tends to reveal things to people only to the degree which they have connection, oversight, influence or authority.

I will outline and illustrate different levels of authority in prophetic revelation

1.Personal realm

Everyone can and should operate on this level. God is able to reveal things concerning your personal life to you such as your gifting and area of calling, the direction for your life in each season and any necessary corrective words from God. You have a right to know everything that God is willing to reveal about you. He is also able to reveal information to you about key people in your life as you keep 'watch over your life'.

Dangerous People

You can act as a watchman over your life and pick up information supernaturally about the affairs of your life. As a watchman over your own personal life, God can for example give dreams to reveal and warn of people who are close to us who have hidden and dangerous agendas. Many of us embrace and draw people close to us and our families without knowing or understanding where they are in their hearts. Some people live amongst us as friends but have the heart and intentions of an enemy. God knows the thoughts and the hearts of men and will sometimes release the spirit of revelation or discernment upon us to help us discern who is good or evil. As I have prayed, God has revealed to me through dreams on different occasions people who were close to me who were stealing from me, lying to me or betraying me. On one occasion, God revealed to a 10 year old girl that some one I had considered a close friend was stabbing me in the back. This was eventually confirmed a few months later.

2"And the natives showed us unusual kindness; for they kindled a fire

and made us all welcome, because of the rain that was falling and because of the cold.

3 But when Paul had <u>gathered a bundle of sticks</u> and laid them on the fire, <u>a viper came out</u> <u>because of the heat</u> and fastened on his hand." –
Acts 28:2-3

Like Paul in the passage above, many people "gather a bundle of sticks (people)" believing them to be friends but it takes the fire of the Holy Spirit through his prophetic revelation to expose the real heart and motives of such people and to destroy their evil plans before they hatch.

2. Family realm

As you were born into a family, you have a stake in that family. Things that happened in that family in the past, present or future will affect you directly, so it is within your right to know what has happened in the past to your forebears, what is happening in the present to any of your siblings or what is in the future for any of your children or their children.

A number of months ago, I had a dream that armed robbers broke into my family home twice. As I woke up from my sleep to ponder upon the meaning of the dream, my 9 year old son ran into my room saying he had a dream that armed robbers broke into our home.

Two weeks later we discovered robbers broke into my wife's family home in Nigeria armed with guns. God revealed this to my son and me at our residence because we are a part of that family either by marriage or birth and we had a right to know. Perhaps if we had prayed harder and more accurately about it, we could have prevented it but no lives were lost.

3. Church realm

God will reveal secret things concerning parishioners to their pastor in order to bring correction or intervention or to provoke intercession on issues concerning them. It is within his jurisdiction as pastor to know the state of his flock and to help them.

God could also reveal a thing about one parishioner to another so they can intervene because they are members of the same family and we are called to be our brother's keeper.

4. Neighbourhood

Revelation could also come to someone who lives within a community concerning a dangerous individual or a dangerous situation within that community because they have a stake within that community. As members of that community, they have the relational and positional authority to speak or pray into the situation.

5. City realm

This realm involves a person who has
1. Positional authority within the city
2. A prophetic mantle or influence over that city
3. An intercessor with the spiritual authority to deal with the issues concerning that city.

I have travelled into certain cities and God has sometimes casually revealed secret things happening in the spirit realm or political realm within that city. About 11 years ago, a certain notable prophet and intercessor was passing through Tallahassee, Florida and had a dream. In the dream, he saw a major contention between a blue side and a red side and he heard a voice saying give it to the "Reds". He did not understand the dream at the time, but he shared it with the pastor who hosted him. A few months later, it became clear what the dream was about as the decision concerning who would be the next President of the United States hung between George W. Bush and Al Gore. It was a tight race and Tallahassee, Florida was the key city in determining who would become the next president of America. A few obscure technicalities led to the decision being made in favour of the "Red" side, the Republicans.

I believe God revealed these things to a passing prophet because he has the authority to tap into that realm and overhear such conversations in the spiritual realm. However, such a prophet has the duty to reveal the information to the pastors who are resident in that city because they have a stake in that city and a burden for it.

6. National realm
God reveals things at a national level to those called as prophets and intercessors to that nation or people who have relationship with them e.g. God revealed the innocence of Jesus to Pontius Pilate's wife and she was able to caution him not to have anything to do with judging Jesus (Matthew 27:24) .Another biblical example of a National prophet is Joseph who was called to the nation of Israel. Such prophets are usually able to speak to kings and those in authority or may be called to preside over one or two spheres of society e.g. politics, economy, family, media or education.

God also reveals things of national concern to others who have a burden for a nation or have a leadership role in one of its communities or a key connection to the nation. God has revealed many things to me concerning the nations of Nigeria and the United Kingdom, but I don't remember him revealing any thing to me concerning Japan or Australia because I don't have a burden for or a stake in those nations.

Call to Pray for the U.K
One morning, I woke up early to pray and fellowship with the Lord as I usually do. As I wrote the day's date in my journal, 05-04-05, the Holy Spirit impressed on me that 05-05-05 was in a month's time and that I needed to pray seriously concerning that day. When I went down stairs about 4 hours later and turned on the TV to hear the news of the day I saw the Prime Minister at the time, Tony Blair declare that
05-05-05 had been declared the day for the general elections. I was totally awestruck by God because that was also the name of someone close to me whose middle name is Joseph (the name of the Prime Minister in bible times) I believed that this was a prophetic sign from God and we responded by raising a prayer chain and making declarations concerning the elections.

In another instance we embarked on a 40 day fast for the nation as a church, which ended on 07/07/07. Around this time, we were also involved in a prayer meeting in our Borough town hall to pray for our Borough (County). Co-ordinated prayers were made in all the town halls across the 33 boroughs in London.

During this time, a child in our church who had no idea what had been going on shared a dream he had had. In his dream, he saw Nelson's column being cleaned at Trafalgar square, Big Ben being polished at Westminster and the walls of Buckingham palace being repainted. It struck me that this was God revealing a prophetic word for the city through this child. The child had seen key political symbols being cleaned or renovated. Big Ben represents the seat of political power in the United Kingdom, Buckingham palace is the seat of Royal power and Nelsons column represents Britain's military power whilst Trafalgar square is the centre point of London.

As I pondered on the dream, I thought 'Could it be that God was revealing these things concerning cleaning, polishing and repainting these key monuments in the heart of this nations capital, on a day that marked exactly 2 years since terrorists bombings in order to bring our attention to some things?' It seemed that God was saying that renewal was coming to the city in the light of the sacrifices that had been made through the prayer efforts.

Also, in prophetic language, cleaning, polishing and repainting could mean a call for repentance to cleanse the nation and prevent future judgement. It could also signify some kind of cleansing from the defilement caused by the deeds of people previously in leadership.

13 ""When I shut up heaven and there is no rain, or command the locusts to devour the land, or send pestilence among My people,
*14 "if My people who are called by My name will humble themselves and pray and seek My face and **turn from their wicked ways,** then I will hear from heaven and will forgive their sin and heal their land." – 2 Chronicles 7:13-14*

God wants to cleanse our hearts and restore us fully such that wrong actions no longer defile or ruin our beautiful land. God revealed issues of great national concern to a child in response to spiritual watch activities of adults.

7. Global realm
A few prophets have the authority and influence that spans continents. Biblical examples of this are people like Daniel, Jeremiah and John the Revelator whom God spoke to about issues on a global stage. Contemporary examples are Rick Joyner, John

Paul Jackson, Bill Hamon and Chuck Pierce. These men also have the authority to speak into and intervene in issues that concern other nations because God has given them oversight over the nations.

Forty days before the July 7th bombing in London, England, God revealed to Chuck Pierce while he was in transit at a London airport that there was a sword of judgement hanging over the U.K and that the spirit holding the sword would be revealed in 40 days. Talk about prophetic precision. To see more details concerning this prophetic word please see the transcript at the end of this chapter.

4 "Then the word of the LORD came to me, saying:
5 "Before I formed you in the womb I knew you; before you were born I sanctified you; I ordained you a prophet to the nations."
6 Then said I: "Ah, Lord GOD! Behold, I cannot speak, for I am a youth."" –Jer. 1:4-6

This was the letter sent out by Chuck Pierce on July 7th 2005
Dear Friends:
I was awakened this morning at 4:30am, unable to breath. Around 5am, the Lord told me to turn on the television and watch the news. I had been praying about our trip to England that I leave on this afternoon. When I turned on the news, Tony Blair was making the statement that London has been attacked by terrorists. The underground transportation network and bus network in central London had been suspended due to several bombings. Actually, the bus that was shown on the news that had been attacked was very close to the hotel we are scheduled to stay in.

Below is the word I gave 40 days ago concerning London and Great Britain. If you remember, when we returned from Nigeria in late

May, the Lord had us stop in London overnight and I spoke at a County Tour meeting in London County. I gave a very detailed word that within 40 days the nation would change. You can read the details from this report below. TODAY IS THE 40th DAY!

When I was in England in May 2004, I gave a word about an 18 month window for the realignment of that nation. This realignment would set the course to determine the next seven years of spiritual activity. In that word, the Lord said, "Do not resist in this season of war. Raise your shield of faith high. Do not become complacent and sympathetic with the enemy that is in your land. If you do, your land will be overtaken - Governmental and social banquets should be watched carefully." I believe the G8 Gathering that is going on in Scotland is very strategic to change a course of world finance. This bombing occurred at the beginning of that gathering.

We are returning to England because a gathering has been scheduled to begin today in London. This meeting is called AWAKEN. The purpose is to change the course of their nation. This meeting is hosted by Rod and Julie Anderson and runs from tonight through the 10th. They share, "In an environment where for a few days we can all gather to pray and seek God, with no agenda and no concrete schedule, we believe the synergy that takes place could birth much insight if we will have ears to hear. To create this atmosphere, we need to pray and depend on God to awaken people's hearts to the 'Now Move' of the Spirit of God. God's word is all truth, but then there is the 'present truth' that the Lord wants us established in (2 Peter 1:12)." Other speakers include Dutch Sheets and Tom & Jane Hamon. The team travelling with me consists of Dutch Sheets, Marty Cassady, Ginny Marks, Robert & Linda Heidler, Joe & Vonnie Askins and Brian Kooiman. Then on Sunday night (July 10), I will be ministering at a citywide gathering in Belfast, Northern Ireland. In light of the upcoming marches (Protestant versus Catholic) that are scheduled to begin there next week, this is a key time to see the Body of Christ arise in a new way in Northern Ireland.

In a separate email, I will be sending out the clear word that came forth in the most recent Tuesday morning prayer meeting that I lead. This is probably one of the most incredible words that I have received from heaven to direct us for this season. So be watching for this word. The Lord began by saying, "Many people are trying to use old methods of warfare to win the war they are in. The only way you will win the war from this point forth is through violent praise. You cannot win any other way. If you do not shift now, you will not be able to see the nations shift. I am sending you back to the root of this nation. Shift the root through violent praise. This is the time to open up the window of your future. Do not go backward. For in the next 10 days if you retreat then you will see the window of your future close, you will find yourself on the wrong side of Jordan and your promise will not be able to be maintained." I will send the complete word by the end of the day. Blessings,
Chuck D. Pierce

****

London Report (May 29, 2005)
As we were waiting in London for our flight to Nigeria, we looked out the windows and saw an interesting pattern in the clouds. There was clearly a sword emblazoned in white across the sky. We knew the Lord was communicating about the SWORD that had come into the atmosphere over London and England. At last night's meeting in London, I explained how this is a year of signs in the sky. Not only did we see this when we were coming through

England on our way to Nigeria, but also <u>when we arrived back in London </u>for our overnight stay. The picture over our desk in our hotel room was a picture of London. The sky in this picture was the formation of a sword where <u>two jets had intersected their contrails.</u>

Sharon Stone is leading a prayer effort across England to gather God's people and pray in every county. This is very similar to what Dutch Sheets and I did in America as we went from state to state in our nation. God had sovereignly ordained us to be in England for a layover so we could be a part of the historic Middlesex County gathering in London. (We met in the heart of this area that hosts the financial and governmental capitals of the United Kingdom.) <u>There is a structural weakness that God is addressing in the system of government in the U.K.</u> If God does not intervene now, England will be absorbed by the European Union. As these groups of intercessors meet from county to county (this was their seventh county meeting) the atmosphere in that nation is beginning to change. (I know that Martin Scott and other groups are also praying throughout England at this time.)

I explained that we "saw a sword in the heavens over London and England." I then led the people to ask "what does this mean at this time?" I explained prophetically that any vision or supernatural phenomenon must be interpreted in light of the Word of God. In the Word of God, <u>a sword can have the following meanings: war, pending judgment,</u> a malicious tongue bringing division, the power of truth, a weapon linked with the armour of God or a piece of armour used in warfare to produce victory. I went back and shared various scenarios from the Word of God linked with the sword. I explained how Jesus in Matthew 10:34 stated, "Think not that I have come to seek peace on earth: <u>I came not to send peace, but a sword.</u>" I shared that this was a time that <u>the sword was being awakened in the atmosphere over London.</u>

One chapter of importance that began to surface was Numbers 14. This is the chapter where Israel refuses to enter Canaan and Moses begins to intercede for the people. I concentrated on two verses. Number 14:3, where the congregation cries out saying, "Why has the Lord brought us to this land to fall by the sword, that our wives and children should become victims? Would it not be better for us to return to Egypt?" They actually tried to elect leadership that would take them "back" to their familiar captivity. The other scripture was Numbers 14:43, "For the Amalekites and Canaanites are there before you and you shall fall by the sword; because you have turned away from the LORD, the LORD will not be with you." I shared that I could hear the Lord saying that this was a critical time and THE NEXT 40 DAYS could determine the reversal of the power of unbelief that was holding the Church captive in that nation. This was the chapter where the people were punished after they were not willing to go to war when they saw the giants in the land. I felt the Lord saying He wanted to take a sword and cut from them the power of unbelief and passivity and the fear to war for their inheritance.

However, I ended with Joshua 5. I saw a tremendous pattern that God was trying to bring forth. This chapter includes 1.) The concept of crossing over to advance toward your inheritance, 2.) Circumcision or cutting away, of the reproach linked with your past captivity and unbelief, 3.) The provisional change from manna to eating the produce of the new land and 4.) The visitation of the Man of heaven with the drawn sword.
I reminded them that I saw the sword in the heavens over London, but did not see what hand was holding and guiding it at this time. I decreed that tradition would not guide the Church from this day forward. I also decreed that false religion (the sword of Islam) would not be able to be the guiding force over England. From this

passage, I felt like God was saying, "I want to take charge over England and London for this hour. I want to be the Commander in Chief over how you progress forward from this day on. <u>I want to transfer a new power over you so you can face that which has been invincible in your past. Contend for My sword to begin to lead you in victory against the giants that you have been unwilling to face in the past. This is your time.</u>"

Please continue to pray for London. Once I gave this word, Brian reminded me that at the end of the 40 days we would leave again from America and be in London for three days of meetings in July. Pray with me during this crucial time.

****

England Report (May 16, 2004)
Many of you who will be reading this report have roots of inheritance here in England. I believe it's very important we pray for England at this time. The team and I found it very interesting that the burden of the Lord came on us in England more than the other two countries we have been in. As a team, we met to pray before I spoke that afternoon, after I spoke and then before I spoke again that night. We felt it was very important that we hear the Lord's message for this nation. Dr. Sharon Stone, with Christian International Europe, is doing a great work here in this country. However, <u>the country, overall, is very weak prophetically.</u> We stayed at the Westwood Training and Conference Center in Coventry where the meeting was being held. The architectural design had allowed for the middle of the Conference Center to reflect "the eye." Of course, many of you know that I have been studying the evil eye and how it affects our lives. This eye is linked with Mammon, superstition, occult and false worship. Before the

meeting began my right eye turned bright red. During our prayer meeting the same thing happened to Marty's eye. After the afternoon session, the Eagles of God team members went and stood under "the eye" and declared the Glory of the Throne Room would penetrate down through the heavens and remove any evil watchers in the region. We formed a cross in the center of the eye and declared the blood of Jesus would cover and block all the workings of the enemy.

When I got to the meeting on Friday afternoon, Sharon stood up before the crowd and said, "We don't want to hear a good preacher. We want to hear the message of God for England." I began by exhorting them the following way: "Prophets in England, you've got your work set out before you. You are in a difficult time. This is a season when prophets need to meet together, worship, cry out and press into revelation. The enemy has a plan to suppress the vision of God in this land. Do not get discouraged. You need to keep saying what needs to be said even if it seems no one in this land is listening."
Then the Lord began to speak,

"There is an unholy alliance being negotiated now in this nation. This alliance will be devastating to this nation in days ahead. This is a very formative time for the future of this nation. I have worked in times past to prevent this nation from forming this type of alliance. However, now it will be your choice whether you align wrongly or align with Me. I say to the people of England, you will be contending concerning this alliance. Prophets need to contend. Intercessors need to contend. Apostles need to rise up. This is a time of choice. I will be sure that My message is heard in this land so the choice is clearly determined. Two prophets in this land will go into high places of governmental authority to tell them the dangers of this wrong alignment. For if this alignment takes place, in five years you will be overtaken by false gods. You are on the verge of being overtaken now. However, there is still time to choose Me. You have three years of choice that will set your course and determine your direction for the next seven years. I am raising up the intercessory call in this nation. Watchman must have a single eye in the land. This is not a time for divided minds and double mindedness. I will offer an opportunity for this land to align with My covenant people, Israel. However, if they reject this alignment they will find another alignment with Germany and France at their door. Syria will also be a part of this wrongful alliance and coalition. England, you have a choice. FOR THE NEXT 18 MONTHS a window of opportunity to change this alignment has been positioned over this nation. I am calling My people in this nation into a time of worship to create portals that My Glory and favour can enter into the nation and bring My choice of life. There is a sound in England that is like none other in My people. Join that sound with My sound from heaven now and this sound will begin to cover and permeate into high places in this nation. If you will allow worship to develop in a new way in this nation, My presence will begin to rule in a new way throughout the land. Join your present sound of intimacy and exaltation of Me with My sound of war. Do not just sing these songs with your mouth but allow the message of these songs to pierce and activate your spirit man for war. I am forming doors in heaven. As you worship, these doors will move into the earth realm and give you opportunity to enter in and present My message to this land. I am calling you to celebrate in a way that your enemies come to My table. I am preparing a table before you and anointing your shield for war. Do not resist in this season of war. Raise your shield of faith high. Do not become complacent and sympathetic with the enemy that is in your land. If you do, your land will be overtaken. Watch the key banquets that are occurring in this land. Governmental and social banquets should be watched carefully.

Prepare the way for Me to enter in and move during these banquets," saith the Lord. "I will give prophets and intercessors and the watchmen of this land favour in these 18 months. From the center of this land a gate is being formed. Determine at this gate whether hell will rule or I will rule," saith the Lord. "The rulership at the gate of England is being determined now."

We are in a seven year war season. Seasons are determined by God. It is amazing to see how nations are aligning in war. In this third year of the seven year war season, alignments are becoming very clear. Choices are being made. During August of this year [2004] economic decisions and change will begin to occur. Autumn is an important time for incredible new beginnings in the earth realm in the way we process and gain our supply for the future. A new anointing for administration is coming into God's people. We will begin to administrate as Joseph did. Joseph gained authority and understanding over the agricultural realm, livestock, land and the people of that day. We are entering into different times of administration. These times may become hard in the natural, but God has a plan for us to multiply. England is at a door of choice on how they will begin to move into this season which sets the course for their future.

Thank you for being a part of this trip with us.

Blessings,

Chuck D. Pierce

CHAPTER 13

PROPHETIC WARNINGS

BLOW THE TRUMPET, SOUND THE ALARM

As mentioned in the previous chapter, the role of the watchman is to pick up what is in the offing and sound the alarm so that concerned parties are warned and prepared to avert disaster or alerted of good news that they also need to prepare for. To demonstrate how this works out in practice, I will outline a few prophetic words and visions which the Lord gave me as a watchman intercessor to proclaim, warn and prepare the body of Christ to respond appropriately.

Ostrich Church and Islamic invasion

As shared earlier in the book, approximately 21 years ago I had a vision of the church illustrated by Ostrich with its head buried in the sand. This mother ostrich began to lay 12 eggs around the circumference of a circle where it stood in the middle of the desert.

As I looked up, I saw an army of invaders approaching from some oil rich countries in the Middle East who planned to destroy the baby ostriches that had just been hatched. However, the mother ostrich was totally oblivious to all that was happening.

I think it is quite instructive that God chose to use a bird like the proverbial ostrich, with its *"head buried in the sand"* to describe the church in this vision. The proverbial ostrich is a bird that is totally oblivious to what is happening around it in spite of near and present danger.

In another trance I had, I heard a voice say that if I didn't interpret this particular ostrich vision my head would 'roll'. I believe this vision is about the state of the Church today. It speaks of current events happening around us which now affect us and will affect future generations if we do not address or deal with. Further, I believe in particular that the vision speaks about the growth and advancement of extremist, fundamentalist Islam and its direct impact and attack on the church and nations in due course if the churches do not rise up into their prophetic role as Watchman Intercessors for the nations and communities they are located in.

The Fall and Public disgrace of Pastors and Politicians

After we hosted a very successful conference themed, "Money, Sex & Power" in July 2001, I went off to a remote location in Bath on a prayer retreat. I chose a location that was remote and far removed from anyone I might know. On one of the nights, by divine appointment and Godly coincidence, I ran into an old wise mentor of mine who lives in Nigeria and was at the hotel for the same reasons - rest and quiet. He informed me that our meeting was not a coincidence and that God was looking for men who would present themselves blameless to God so that He can use them for His glory. I shared with Him that on my 2 hour drive to Bath, I was listening to a sermon where the preacher kept re-emphasising the phrase, "Walk before Me and be thou blameless".

1"When Abram was ninety-nine years old, the LORD appeared to Abram and said to him, "I am Almighty God; walk before Me and be blameless.
2 "And I will make My covenant between Me and you and will multiply you exceedingly."
3 Then Abram fell on his face and God talked with him, saying:
4 "As for Me, behold, My covenant is with you and you shall be a father of many nations." Genesis 17:1-4

After leaving this gentleman, I began to ponder upon what he had said. I went back to my hotel room and turned on the TV to watch the news. One of the news stories was about the famous author and politician Jeffery Archer; he had just been jailed for perjury in a case in which he had been caught soliciting for sex from a prostitute. God immediately spoke to me that we would begin to see this kind of public disgrace with Pastors on 24 hour national and international news.

Unfortunately, a couple of years later, pastors began to be jailed for misconduct of various kinds. From America to London, pastor's financial and sexual misconducts were broadcast on the news and many faced jail sentences and the destruction of the ministries that they had been building their whole lives. It is a difficult subject and I did spend some time debating whether or not to include this section, but it is important to declare that God did warn of these matters and revealed what was to come. I am sure that I was not the only one that God spoke to about these matters in an attempt to stave off disgrace and discredit to His word and work.

Storms are coming!
One of the most defining encounters of my prophetic journey is a visitation I had in January 2005 where God showed me that a

season and series of storms were coming which would devastate and shake many foundations. I responded by preaching it as a warning message at church which was recorded and broadcast. When the same message was played 5 years later every word spoken had literally come to pass.

Since the word was given, we have witnessed various kinds of storms in different places. We have had physical storms like Hurricane Katrina, the Haiti and Japanese earthquakes and Tsunami. We have seen unprecedented financial storms and crashes in the financial and property markets on a global scale, with many people experiencing major personal losses. We have also witnessed various scandals in the ministry, politics and banking arena involving Christians. We have seen major marital storms with the recent spate of divorces of high profile ministers and pastors. We have also witnessed in recent times, the sudden death and loss of some high profile ministers or their wives which have rocked the faith of many. Many can also recount storms of a more personal nature that have affected them deeply.

The evil wind did blow according to the Word of the Lord, but could it have been averted? I believe some of them could have been averted with the concerted and extensive prayers of a concert of people.

Pray against the spirit of Divorce
While I was praying at a vigil on the 30th of December 2008, I had a strong impression in my spirit to pray seriously against the "spirit of divorce". At the time, I did not take the message very seriously because until then in the church I pastured, which had been in existence for 12 years, we had very few divorces; I could only remember one or two divorces happening since our inception as a church.

About 8 months after the strong impression, I began to see attacks on marriages inside and outside our congregation of demonic proportions. I began to learn of people who I knew to be strong Christians who had yielded to extra marital affairs or who were getting divorced. A few more months down the line, we began to notice a number of high profile ministers filing for divorce. I believe this is an attack and onslaught of the enemy which was revealed and could have been averted or minimised by prophetic intercession.

These prophetic messages are not meant to scare us or be fodder for gossip. They are divine alerts to get us praying to prevent them from coming to pass. We have noticed in particular as we prayed concertedly regarding marriages and supported failing marriages with counselling and teaching that divorces have been prevented and families have been able to stay intact.

We now have a team of women at church praying regularly for marriages, those believing for conception, as well as those who are already pregnant. They also pray regularly for children and teenagers to be delivered from the plans of the enemy. These women share warning dreams or words that they have had from God and disarm the enemy in prayer. This is the role of the watchman and the calling of the church. In the next chapter we will look in more detail at prayer in the life of the prophetic person.

CHAPTER 14

A PROPHET'S INTERCESSION AND SPIRITUAL WARFARE

Prophetic Intercession is the intervention by an individual and interception of another who is being attacked or held captive by the enemy, after the attack has being made known by prophetic insight and revelation. This is done by the use of prayers, declarations, commands and various other supernatural legislative acts to restrain the enemies' assaults or to wrestle the powers of darkness for the release of captives, victims, objects and possessions.

A great example of intercession is when David intervened when a lion took a lamb out of his flock to devour but he went on to pursue the lion and wrestle the lamb from the lion and out of the jaws of death.

34"But David said to Saul, "Your servant used to <u>keep his father's</u> <u>sheep</u> and <u>when a lion or a bear came</u> and <u>took a lamb out of the flock</u>,
35 I <u>went out after it</u> and <u>struck it</u> and <u>delivered the lamb from its</u> <u>mouth</u>; and when it arose against me, I caught it by its beard and struck and killed it.
36 "Your servant has killed both lion and bear; and this uncircumcised Philistine will be like one of them, seeing he has defied the armies of the living God.""-1 Sam. 17:34-36*

Praying Targeted Prayers

When interceding for an individual, we should use the same process that David did to deliver the lamb out of the lion's mouth. We intercede by:

1. Stepping in on behalf of the person we are interceding for Striking the enemy
2. Snatching the one we are interceding for from its mouth
3. The prayers must be specific, targeted and skilful in order to be effective.

Abraham is another great example of an act of intercession, as he negotiated with God to save Sodom and Gomorrah from impending destruction.

17"And the LORD said, "<u>Shall I hide from Abraham what I am doing,</u>
18 "since Abraham shall surely become a great and mighty nation and all the nations of the earth shall be blessed in him?... 20 And the LORD said, "<u>Because the outcry against Sodom and Gomorrah is great and</u> <u>because their sin is very grave,</u>
21 "I will go down now and see whether they have done altogether according to the outcry against it that has come to Me; and if not, I will know."
22 Then <u>the men turned away from there and went toward Sodom</u>, but <u>Abraham still stood before the LORD.</u>

23 And Abraham came near and said, <u>"Would You also destroy the righteous with the wicked?</u>

24 "Suppose there were fifty righteous within the city; would You also destroy the place and not spare it for the fifty righteous that were in it?

25 "Far be it from You to do such a thing as this, to slay the righteous with the wicked, so that the righteous should be as the wicked; far be it from You! Shall not the Judge of all the earth do right?"

26 So the LORD said, "If I find in Sodom fifty righteous within the city, then I will spare all the place for their sakes."

27 Then Abraham answered and said, "Indeed now, I who am but dust and ashes have taken it upon myself to speak to the Lord:

28 "Suppose there were five less than the fifty righteous; would You destroy all of the city for lack of five?" So He said, "If I find there forty-five, I will not destroy it."

29 And he spoke to Him yet again and said, "Suppose there should be forty found there?" So He said, "I will not do it for the sake of forty."

30 Then he said, "Let not the Lord be angry and I will speak: Suppose thirty should be found there?" So He said, "I will not do it if I find thirty there."

31 And he said, "Indeed now, I have taken it upon myself to speak to the Lord: Suppose twenty should be found there?" So He said, "I will not destroy it for the sake of twenty."

32 Then he said, "Let not the Lord be angry and I will speak but once more: Suppose ten should be found there?" And He said, "I will not destroy it for the sake of ten."

33 So the LORD went His way as soon as He had finished speaking with Abraham; and Abraham returned to his place. - Gen18:18-33

19:1 Now the two angels came to Sodom in the evening and <u>Lot was sitting in the gate of Sodom.</u> When Lot saw them, he rose to meet them and he bowed himself with his face toward the ground."- Gen. 19:1

In this instance, we can see that Abraham pleaded for and negotiated for the release of captives. He did so by appealing to God's merciful nature. Likewise, we can intercede for people who are lawful captives or suffering due to their own actions – imploring and negotiating with God for release because of His kindness.

The Weapons of our Warfare

3"For though we walk in the flesh, <u>we do not war according to the flesh.</u> 4 For <u>the weapons of our warfare</u> are not carnal but mighty in God for <u>pulling down strongholds,"</u> – 2 Corinth. 10:3-4

As a prophetic intercessor, it is one thing to be able to receive supernatural revelation concerning an impending tragedy, but it is another thing to have the authority, tools and the skill to avert it through intercession in prayer. In prophetic intercession, we have tools and keys to help in winning our battles, just as we have tools or weapons to receive prophetic revelation. I will outline and discuss some of the tools, weapons or keys for restraining the enemy and releasing captives from his hold below.

Prayers

Prayer is a very important key or weapon in intercession and breaking down spiritual strongholds in order to release the oppressed and people bound in spiritual captivity.

There are various kinds of prayers such as petitions, supplication, intercession, thanksgiving and declarations. When the demonic spirit at work has been discerned and prayers of intercession have been made, the next thing to do is to exercise our authority in Christ by making decrees and by verbal declarations from the word of God. This can be done in a deliverance session when the individual is present or by sending the word of God by faith to free someone who is not present.

"He <u>sent His word</u> and <u>healed them</u> and <u>delivered them</u> from <u>their</u> <u>destructions</u>."
Psalm 107:20

Before we look at intercession in more detail further down, it's important to talk a little about the spiritual realm and spiritual authority as these are key in intercession.

Preventing and cancelling demonic attacks and assignments
The best way to avoid destruction is to prevent it.

A Day in heaven (the spiritual realm)
This set of scriptures below is fascinating because it gives us insight into what happens in the "heavenlies". As we read it we come to understand that assemblies take place in heaven where matters on earth and the issues of life are discussed.

"6 <u>Now there was a day </u>when the sons of God came to present themselves before the LORD and Satan also came among them.
7 And the LORD said to Satan, "From where do you come?" So Satan answered the LORD and said, "From going to and fro on the earth and from walking back and forth on it."
8 Then the LORD said to Satan, "Have you considered My servant Job, that there is none like him on the earth, a blameless and upright man, one who fears God and shuns evil?"
9 So Satan answered the LORD and said, "Does Job fear God for nothing?
10 "Have You not made a hedge around him, around his household and around all that he has on every side? You have blessed the work of his hands and his possessions have increased in the land.
11 "But now, stretch out Your hand and touch all that he has and he

will surely curse You to Your face!"

*12 And the LORD said to Satan, <u>"Behold, all that he has is in your</u>
<u>power; only do not lay a hand on his person.</u>" So Satan went out from
the presence of the LORD."- Job 1:6-12*

The Day on Earth (the physical realm)

As a result of the discussion in the heavenly realm, Satan was
given limited powers which would drastically affect Job's life on
earth. In this passage, we see how power and authority granted
in the spiritual realm affects the natural realm.

*"13 <u>Now there was a day</u> when his sons and daughters were eating and
drinking wine in their oldest brother's house;*

*14 and a messenger came to Job and said, "The oxen were ploughing
and the donkeys feeding beside them,*

*15 "when the Sabeans raided them and took them away-indeed they
have killed the servants with the edge of the sword; and I alone have
escaped to tell you!"*

*16 While he was still speaking, another also came and said, "The fire
of God fell from heaven and burned up the sheep and the servants and
consumed them; and I alone have escaped to tell you!"*

*17 While he was still speaking, another also came and said, "The
Chaldeans formed three bands, raided the camels and took them away,
yes and killed the servants with the edge of the sword; and I alone have
escaped to tell you!"*

*18 While he was still speaking, another also came and said, "Your sons
and daughters were eating and drinking wine in their oldest brother's
house,*

*19 "and suddenly a great wind came from across the wilderness and
struck the four corners of the house and it fell on the young people and
they are dead; and I alone have escaped to tell you!"*

*20 Then Job arose, tore his robe and shaved his head; and he fell to the
ground and worshiped.*

21 And he said: "Naked I came from my mother's womb and naked shall I return there. The LORD gave and the LORD has taken away; Blessed be the name of the LORD."
22 In all this Job did not sin nor charge God with wrong." – Job 1:13-22

Job's story is important because it helps us to understand some key things.
Satan's powers are limited – just as God gave Satan boundaries by His words - so can we.
Just as decisions in the spiritual realm can affect the earthly realm, earthly decisions can affect the spiritual realm, so let's utilise the authority that we have been given in prayer. We can restrain the forces of darkness and prevent destruction by discerning their plans and giving them quarantine before they are hatched.

*"I will give you the keys of the kingdom of heaven; whatever you **bind** on earth will be bound in heaven and whatever you **loose** on earth will be **loose**d in heaven."*
Matthew 16:19

Even though testing's and tough times come, God's ultimate plan for us is good and when we can sit out opposition, we will eventually have victory.

With this in mind, now let's look at intercession in some more depth.

Declarations
When we declare what scripture says over people's lives and situation even when the circumstances seem contrary, the situation will eventually align to God's will.

A number of years ago, I received a call from the father of a member of our church. He inform me that he had spoken to his daughter a few minutes prior and noticed that she was incoherent and feared for her sanity. I went to the daughter's house and discovered that she was indeed mentally unwell – she didn't know her own name or who I was and was illogical and confused. I prayed for her, declaring God's word over her life and declaring the sound mind she had in Christ. She was set free and became totally lucid again because we declared the Word of God over her.

26"For then you will have your delight in the Almighty and lift up your face to God.

27 You will *make your prayer to Him*, He will hear you and you will pay your vows.

28 You will *also declare a thing* and it will be *established for you*; so light will shine on your ways.

29 When they cast you down and you say, *'Exaltation will come!' Then He will save the humble person.*

30 He will even *deliver one who is not innocent*; Yes, he will be delivered by the purity of your hands." " – Job 22:26-30

Pronouncements

This is similar to a declaration but it happens when a declaration is made in faith for example by saying that in certain number of days certain things will happen to align with God's will, His Word and His way.

15 "So he said, "Call her." When he had called her, she stood in the doorway.

16 Then he said, "*About this time next year you shall embrace a son.*" And she said, "No, my lord. Man of God, do not lie to your maidservant!"

17 But <u>the woman conceived and bore a son when the appointed time had come,</u> of which Elisha had told her." – 2 Kings 4:15-17

This scripture brings to mind an incident when the son of a church member fell into a coma after an injury on a basketball court. The parents were very anxious as could be expected as they had been told there was no way to know when he would recover or what state he would be in if he did. On my arrival at the hospital, I felt impressed to lay flat on the floor and worship God. As I rose up from that stance of worship, I was divinely inspired by the Lord to make a pronouncement that he would recover speedily and fully. By the next morning, he had come out of the coma and was eating cornflakes unassisted! It was an awesome recovery.

Preaching

22"And they were <u>astonished at His teaching,</u> for He <u>taught them as one having authority</u> and not as the scribes.
23 Now there was <u>a man in their synagogue with an unclean spirit.</u> And he cried out,
24 saying "Let us alone! What have we to do with You, Jesus of Nazareth? Did You come to destroy us? I know who You are--the Holy One of God!"
25 But Jesus rebuked him, saying, "Be quiet and come out of him!"
26 And when <u>the unclean spirit had convulsed him and cried out with a loud voice, he came out of him.</u>
27 Then they were all amazed, so that they questioned among themselves, saying, "What is this? What new doctrine is this? For with authority He commands even the unclean spirits and they obey Him.""
– Mark 1:22-27

The preaching of the undiluted and uncompromised word of God with authority can make demonic spirits uncomfortable and cause them to be exposed and eventually expelled, resulting in the freedom for the oppressed individual. I have on two different occasions witnessed demonic manifestations from people as the word of God was taught – one minute the person was sitting and listening to the word just as I was, the next minute, the person was gyrating and manifesting as the evil spirit at work was provoked by the word. The word of God is powerful! In both instances, a simple declaration of liberty was all it took to seal their deliverance.

Worship

15"And Saul's servants said to him, "Surely, <u>a distressing spirit</u> from God <u>is troubling you.</u>

16 "Let our master now command your servants, who are before you, to <u>seek out a man who is a skilful player on the harp;</u> and it shall be that he will play it with his hand when the distressing spirit from God is upon you and you shall be well."

17 So Saul said to his servants, "Provide me now a man who can play well and bring him to me."" – 1 Sam. 16:15-17

Praise and worship is a very powerful weapon in the arsenal of a believer. It goes over and above what prayers alone will do. I have gotten into the habit of worshiping extensively at the end of some services (after those who need to hurry home to lunch have left the service). On these occasions, God always speaks. On a certain Sunday service, I saw (in the spirit) a couple who had been handcuffed by two separate demons and were being pulled apart in different directions. Shortly after I declared it, the wicked spirit lifted a young lady from her seat and she began to walk aggressively towards me at the pulpit. The spirit spewed out vile threats in a man's voice threatening to destroy her. As we continued worshiping, she ran towards a side wall hit her head on the wall and the spirit left her. How do I know that the word was for her and that the spirit left her? Shortly afterwards, her husband from whom she had been estranged for a short time and who was living in another country called her because he wanted to reconcile with her.

Fasting

"14 And when they had come to the multitude, a man came to Him, kneeling down to Him and saying,

15 "Lord, have mercy on my son, for <u>he is an epileptic</u> and <u>suffers severely</u>; for he often <u>falls into the fire</u> and <u>often into the water.</u>

16 "So I brought him to Your disciples, <u>but they could not cure him</u>….. And <u>Jesus rebuked the demon</u> and <u>it came out of him;</u> and the child was cured from <u>that very hour</u>.

19 Then the disciples came to Jesus privately and said, <u>"Why could we not cast it out?"</u>

20 So Jesus said to them, "Because of your unbelief; for assuredly, I say to you, if you have faith as a mustard seed, you will say to this mountain, 'Move from here to there,' and it will move; and nothing will be impossible for you.

21 "However, <u>this kind does not go out except by prayer and fasting</u>."""

Matthew 17:14-16 & 19 -20

The above scriptures show that there are certain stubborn problems that will not respond to many things e.g. prayer or praise alone. The key to breaking through in such situations is to add the weapon of fasting to increase our spiritual potency and sensitivity. Oftentimes, when we have just completed a season of fasting in church, there are many testimonies of deliverance and breakthroughs in various areas.

Prophetic Fulfilment and Delay

12"Then he said to me, "Do not fear, Daniel, for <u>from the first day that</u>

you set your heart to understand and to *humble yourself before your God, your words were heard; and I have come because of your words.*

13 "*But the prince of the kingdom of Persia withstood me twenty-one days; and behold, Michael, one of the chief princes, came to help me, for I had been left alone there with the kings of Persia.*

14 "*Now I have come to make you understand what will happen to your people in the latter days, for the vision refers to many days yet to come.*" " – Dan. 10:12-14

The above passage shows that whenever a person seeks to deliver a message or the fulfilment of a prophetic word declared on earth, there will be dark spiritual forces that seek to resist the delivery of the word from heaven or the performance of the word on earth.

Battle for your Prophecy
When a prophet declares a word, he has the responsibility to ensure that he contends in the place of prayer and with persistence until the word comes into manifestation. Those who receive the word must also play their part. I have seen instances where people received prophetic words that they would conceive and give birth to a child, who either did not conceive at all or suffered a miscarriage and lost the pregnancy. This is proof that the enemy wants to abort or delay the fulfilment of your prophetic word.

When we notice that we are experiencing resistance spiritually or extensive delay, a key strategy is perseverance. We are rarely told in church these days that perseverance is a spiritual tool. We need to employ it and continue to battle until we see results. This is what Daniel did and after twenty one days the angel who had been trying to get to him from day one of his fast was able to breakthrough and get to him.

Birthing your Prophecy
"This charge I commit to you, son Timothy, <u>according to the prophecies</u> previously made concerning you, that by them you may <u>wage the good warfare</u>… " – 2 Tim.1:18

There could also be what seems like a delay in prophecy because the recipient of the prophetic word does not go into the place of prayer to help give birth to the word that was spoken. There should be an effort on the part of the prophet and the recipient of the word to ensure that they do not cease praying until the word is birthed into manifestation.

Times and Seasons
"of the sons of Issachar who had <u>understanding of the times</u>, to <u>know what Israel ought to do</u>"-1 Chronicles 12:32

Some other times, a delay is experienced in prophetic fulfilment because the fulfilment of the prophecy is time sensitive. We see this evidenced in the case of Israel's 70 year captivity in Babylon. No amount of praying could change or shorten the time of captivity to 30 years because the timeframe for the prophetic fulfilment had already been declared by Jeremiah.

2 "In the first year of his reign I, Daniel, understood by the books <u>the number of the years specified</u> by the word of the LORD through Jeremiah the prophet, that <u>He would accomplish seventy years in the desolations of Jerusalem.</u>
3 Then I set my face toward the Lord God to make request by prayer and supplications, with fasting, sackcloth and ashes.
4 And I prayed to the LORD my God," – Daniel 9:2-4

We need to make sure our prayers are in alignment with Gods timetable, schedule and purposes if we want to see results to our prayers. Some prophecies are also conditional upon certain other things happening. Even though God had revealed Joseph's prophetic destiny through a dream (which was a fulfilment of God's promise to his father Isaac and grandfather Abraham) and his father Jacob had given him a coat that distinguished him, the promise to Joseph was not fulfilled until he had been prepared and reformed in character.

Angelic Assistance in Intercession

There is a common adage that states, "Beware of an idea whose time has come!" This is so true when it comes with prophetic words and their fulfilment. When it is the "due time" for a prophecy to come to pass, angels are actually waiting with a readiness to be activated to assist the assignment.

"Then he said to me, "Do not fear, Daniel, for <u>from the first day that you set your heart to understand and</u> to humble yourself before your God, <u>your words were heard;</u> and <u>I have come because of your words</u>." - Dan. 10:12

"Bless the LORD, you <u>His angels,</u> who excel in strength, <u>who do His word</u>, heeding <u>the voice of His word.</u>" – Psalm 103:20

"5 Peter was therefore kept in prison, but <u>constant prayer</u> was offered to God for him by the church.

6 And when Herod was about to bring him out, that night Peter was sleeping, bound <u>with two chains between two soldiers;</u> and the guards before the door were keeping the prison.

7 Now <u>behold, an angel of the Lord stood by him</u> and a light shone in the prison; and he struck Peter on the side and raised him up, saying, "Arise quickly!" And <u>his chains fell off his hands.</u>

8 Then the angel said to him, "Gird yourself and tie on your sandals"; and so he did. And he said to him, "Put on your garment and follow me."

9 So he went out and followed him and <u>did not know that what was done by the angel was real, but thought he was seeing a vision.</u>
10 When they were past the first and the second guard posts, they came to the iron gate that leads to the city, <u>which opened to them of its own accord;</u> and they went out and went down one street and <u>immediately the angel departed from him</u>." – Acts 12:5-10

The angel in the above passage was ready and responded because the seventy year timeframe was fulfilled and he was activated because of the prayers made by Daniel in accordance with God's word concerning Israel. When you have concerted prayer and due time or season working together, the results are always explosive (in a positive way)!

CHAPTER 15

PROPHETS IN THE MARKETPLACE

The Prophetic gift and ministry was not given to be used and demonstrated only in the church arena, it was given by God for the <u>edification</u> of the Church and also for the <u>evangelisation</u> of the world. God gave us gifts not just to solve our problems but to reach and touch others and solve other people's problems.

There are many problems in the world as we have seen in the first few chapters of this book where people are desperately seeking psychics, astrologers and witches for the solution to life's problems. We even saw how the world's leaders such as the one time president of the USA, President Reagan and his Wife Nancy Reagan, more or less had a psychic on their payroll who helped them make decisions involving their personal affairs and also matters of the State. The psychic guided them into choosing George Bush to serve as Reagan's Vice-President.

The Church therefore needs to begin to identify, prepare and position competent and mature prophets who will serve in key positions in government and other spheres of society.

The Call to influence Society
In order to effectively influence society, we must understand what the words "Society" and "Influence" mean.
A general definition of the word "Society" is a group of organised people living together united by common interests.
The word "Influence" simply means the power to affect another or to sway one's decisions or actions.
If the church is going to influence or affect people's decisions and actions, we must be strategically placed amongst them and positioned in such a way as to touch and reach them for God's purposes.

It is generally believed and agreed that there are 7 spheres of society. They are listed as follows;
1. Politics (Government)
2. Media
3. Education
4. Entertainment & Sports
5. Business & Career
6. Religion
7. Family

Marketplace Prophets in the Bible
Scripture is replete with examples of people who were raised and positioned by God in the heart of society (the Marketplace) to bring about Godly reforms and influence e.g. Joseph, Daniel, Esther, Joseph of Arimethia, Lydia of Phillipi the seller of purple, Joana the Wife of Chuza, the Treasurer (Minister of Finance) etc.

Those who have access to Secrets become leaders amongst men
The people of the world generally have no understanding or
respect for godly things, but they will have respect for godly
wisdom when it solves real life problems. The world and its
systems also celebrate, reward and promote people who are
diligent and can deliver results.

Hence, like Joseph and Daniel in a foreign land, we see that those
who have access to Secrets become leaders amongst men and when
they become leaders, they can bring about godly influence in the
realm or sphere of society.

*"8 Now it came to pass in the morning <u>that his spirit was troubled and he</u>
<u>sent and called for all the magicians of Egypt and all its wise men</u>. And
Pharaoh told them his dreams, but <u>there was no one who could interpret</u>
<u>them for Pharaoh.</u>*
*9 Then the chief butler spoke to Pharaoh, saying: "I remember my faults
this day.*
*10 "When Pharaoh was angry with his servants and put me in custody
in the house of the captain of the guard, both me and the chief baker,*
*11 "we each had a dream in one night, he and I. Each of us dreamed
according to the interpretation of his own dream.*
*12 "Now <u>there was a young Hebrew man with us there</u>, a servant of the
captain of the guard. And we told him and <u>he interpreted our dreams for</u>
<u>us;</u> to each man he interpreted according to his own dream.*
*13 "<u>And it came to pass, just as he interpreted for us, so it happened</u>. He
restored me to my office and he hanged him." "- Gen.41:8-13*

We can also see from the above passage that those who have access
to divine secrets can solve humanities problems and stop a national
crisis.

28 "Then Joseph said to Pharaoh, "<u>The dreams of Pharaoh</u> are one; <u>God</u>

has shown Pharaoh what He is about to do:…

….29 "Indeed <u>seven years of great plenty will come throughout all the</u>
<u>*land of Egypt;*</u>

30 "but after them seven years of famine will arise and all the plenty will
be forgotten in the land of Egypt; and the famine will deplete the land.

31 "So the plenty will not be known in the land because of the famine
following, for it will be very severe." Gen. 41:28-31

Joseph the Prophet becomes Prime-Minister

We see that as Joseph was seen as competent in interpreting
Pharaoh's dream and also found to be learned, wise and skilled in
handling the economic affairs of a nation, he was promoted to the
highest office in the nation under Pharaoh.

God is looking for people who will not only just develop their
prophetic gifting and abilities but also for people who will acquire
knowledge and develop skills that are relevant to solving real
problems in society and who will become competent and excellent
at it.

32 "And the dream was repeated to Pharaoh twice because the thing is
established by God and God will shortly bring it to pass.

33 "Now therefore, let Pharaoh select a <u>discerning</u> and <u>wise man</u> and <u>set</u>
<u>*him over the land of Egypt.*</u>

34 "Let Pharaoh do this and <u>let him appoint officers over the land</u>, to
<u>*collect one-fifth of the produce of the land of Egypt in the seven plentiful*</u>
<u>*years.*</u>

35 "And let them gather all the food of those good years that are coming
and store up grain under the authority of Pharaoh and let them keep food
in the cities.

36 "Then that food shall be as a reserve for the land for the seven years of
famine which shall be in the land of Egypt, <u>that the land may not perish</u>
<u>*during the famine*</u>.""
Gen. 41:25-36

I believe the Prophetic gift is a key God has given the church to take its members into the heart of society and the forefront of their field to affect the destiny of nations and influence them for the glory of God.

It is time to arise and take your prophetic place in society!

SOME OTHER PUBLICATIONS
BY DR SOLA FOLA-ALADE

**21 WAYS TO
MIND YOUR
OWN BUSINESS
(VOLUME 1)**

**SO WHO DO YOU
REALLY THINK
YOU ARE?**

**DISCOVER YOUR
HIDDEN
TREASURES**

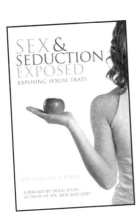

**SEX &
SEDUCTION
EXPOSED**
EXPOSING SEXUAL TRAITS

**12 THINGS YOU
DON'T KNOW THAT
COULD BE
DESTROYING YOU**

**THE LITTLE THINGS
THAT CAN MAKE A
BIG DIFFERENCE IN
YOUR MARRIAGE**

LEADERSHIP & LIFESTYLE MAGAZINE

Visit www.developingleaders.net

DIAGNOSTIC TOOLS
BY DR SOLA FOLA-ALADE

MARRIAGE CHECK UP
How Healthy is Your Marriage?

CHECK THIS OUT AT
WWW.ENJOYYOURMARRIAGE.COM

SPIRITUAL WARFARE PROFILE
(WWW.EMPOWERMENTUNIVERSITY.COM)

AUDIO SERIES
BY DR SOLA FOLA-ALADE

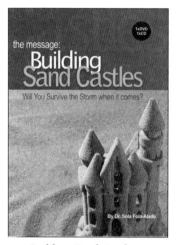

Building Sand Castles
(CD &DVD)

12 Things you don't know that
could be destroying you
(4 x CD)

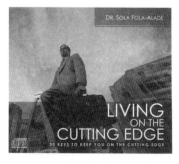

Living on the Cutting Edge
(30 x Mini Sermons)

How To Make A Big Income
From A Small Business; The
Entrepreneurs MBA in One Day
(6x CD)

COMING SOON!

Empowerment University
This is the new vehicle through which all my leadership training & development options in vocation & spiritual endeavours will be conducted?
Please see below or visit empowermentuniversity.com for courses currently available.
For further details or to book sessions please send an email to registrar@empowermentuniversity.com.

12 D'S RETREAT
Experience Empowerment, Freedom, Breakthroughs and Transformation at the 12 Ds Retreat.
The retreat is designed to help you in:
Identifying and breaking negative patterns and trends in your Life & Family
Identifying Deep Wounds and healing them
Discovering and destroying Negative Mindsets
Breaking free from Sinful habits and Addictive behaviour
Exposing and breaking free of Demonic influences

SCHOOL OF PROPHETS
A Six Session programme held once a week which will develop the Seer in you.

DREAM WORKSHOP
A one day workshop that will provide the basis for delegates to understand & interpret the dreams you dream.

DISCOVER YOUR DESTINY WORKSHOP

A 3 session workshop that provides the tools for understanding who you are & where best you will function as well as a guided goal setting session for a sphere of life of your choice eg Career, business, Family, Ministry, Personal etc.

MARRIAGE ENRICHMENT WEEKEND

A weekend away in idyllic surroundings, where couples learn together how their marriages could remain or become heaven on earth!

ENTREPRENEURS CLUB

A 12 session programme held once a week that provides budding & existing Entrepreneurs with the skills required, in starting & sustaining a thriving business.

IMPACT SEMINARS

These are quarterly seminars on topical issues.

DIAGNOSTIC TOOLS

These are various online surveys that will provide a status report of your status on a particular aspect of life. Available on request are:

Capacity Building Test
Spiritual Profile
Marriage Satisfaction Test

We look forward to hosting
you at one of these sessions.